confessions
of a
prayer wimp

Also by Mary Pierce

*When Did I Stop Being Barbie
and Become Mrs. Potato Head?*

mary pierce

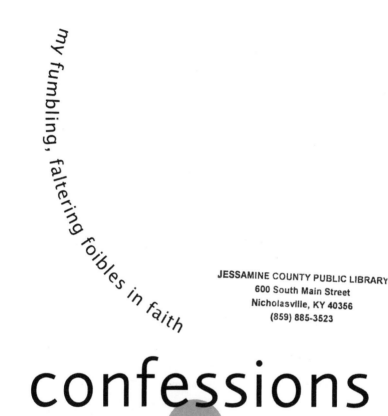

my fumbling, faltering foibles in faith

confessions

of a

prayer wimp

ZONDERVAN™

GRAND RAPIDS, MICHIGAN 49530 USA

We want to hear from you. Please send your comments about this book to us in care of zreview@zondervan.com. Thank you.

ZONDERVAN™

Confessions of a Prayer Wimp
Copyright © 2005 by Mary Pierce

Requests for information should be addressed to:
Zondervan, *Grand Rapids, Michigan 49530*

Library of Congress Cataloging-in-Publication Data

Pierce, Mary, 1949–
    Confessions of a prayer wimp : my fumbling, faltering foibles in faith /
Mary Pierce.
      p. cm.
    ISBN 0-310-24979-1 (softcover)
    1. Pierce, Mary, 1949– 2. Christian biography—United States. I. Title.
BR1725.P5147A3 2005
277.3'093'092—dc22

277,3093
Pier

2004019808

All Scripture quotations, unless otherwise indicated, are taken from the *Holy Bible, New International Version®*. *NIV®*. Copyright © 1973, 1978, 1984 by International Bible Society. Used by permission of Zondervan. All rights reserved.

Scripture quotations marked KJV are taken from the King James Version of the Bible.

Scripture quotations marked NASB are taken from the *New American Standard Bible*, © Copyright 1960, 1962, 1963, 1968, 1971, 1972, 1973, 1975, 1977, 1995 by The Lockman Foundation. Used by permission.

Scripture quotations marked NLT are taken from the *Holy Bible, New Living Translation*, copyright © 1996. Used by permission of Tyndale House Publishers, Inc., Wheaton, IL 60189 USA. All rights reserved.

Published in association with, the literary agency of Alive Communications, Inc., 7680 Goddard St., Suite 200, Colorado Springs, Colorado 80920.

Interior design by Beth Shagene

Printed in the United States of America

04 05 06 07 08 09 10 /❖ DCI/ 10 9 8 7 6 5 4 3 2 1

To Cary
Shalom, sweet sister

contents

part three

finding the way home

acknowledgments

Thanks again to my sweet family—Terry, Alex, Katy, Lizz, Jenny, Laura, and Dan and the rest of the clan—for all the love and support. You are my fogged mirror. Thanks to Mother, Carol, David, Jeff, Janie, and Lollie. You are there, always, and I'm grateful. (Don, how we miss you!)

Thanks to Kathy, John, Lindy, Dan, Wes, Charlene, Jeff, Roxanne, Vicki, Brian, Karen, Charles, Rod, Lil, Joan, Sandi, Karen, Beth, Joann, Deb, and so many other faithful praying friends—warriors all—for blessing me so. Thanks to the cheerleaders in the Western Wisconsin Christian Writers Guild for spurring me on.

Thanks to Sandy Vander Zicht at Zondervan for her patience, insight, and editorial skill and for seeing the silk purse instead of the sow's ear. Thanks to my agent Lee Hough at Alive Communications for his prayers, his fierce dedication, and his astute judgment.

Thanks to my niece Mary Lee Hanson for asking how I got "from there to here." Here is the answer to your question.

Thank you, Book Nook ladies, for parting the curtain. See you in heaven!

introduction

I confess. I am not a deep thinker. Some authors spend pages and pages plumbing the depths of the universe, cosmic mysteries, quantum physics, the space-time continuum, the origins of species, and the miraculous workings of the mind. I'm not one of those authors. I take the universe as it comes, one sunrise at a time.

I'm content to let mysteries remain mysteries. I don't have to understand how electricity works in order to turn on the lamp. I've learned it helps to know where the circuit-breaker box is and how to turn off the juice before you replace an outlet. There's a lesson you don't need twice.

Quantum physics? I have enough trouble with inertia, thank you very much. I don't have any trouble understanding inertia; its properties are painfully obvious every morning when I have to get up. I understand it fine. I just have a little trouble overcoming it.

The space-time continuum? Not my thing. I am content to believe that today will be today and tomorrow will be tomorrow. Time travel can remain the domain of braver souls than I.

Unless I could somehow wind up younger than I really am. Then I might give it a try.

As for our origins, if Darwin wanted to think he came from a monkey, that's fine for him. We've all had moments, haven't we, when we can't imagine how we—so brilliant, so charming, so *normal*—could possibly have come from *our* family? I wonder how Darwin's mom took the news of his theory. Maybe she wondered how she ended up being the only normal one in *her* family.

I'd say Darwin had a little self-image problem. If the choice is accidentally falling out of a monkey's family tree or being created by a loving God, why wouldn't you choose the latter? But what do I know? I'm not an expert in the workings of the human mind, or any other area for that matter.

I have a little knowledge about a few things, but you know what they say about a little knowledge. Dangerous. Very dangerous. When it comes to most things, I'm dumb as a stump. You won't get rocket science from me, or even kitchen science. Most of my ideas are half-baked.

No, I'm not a deep thinker. I've plumbed my own depths and found myself to be quite shallow indeed. Especially in this whole area of the spiritual. I'm no spiritual giant. I'm spiritually puny, just a wimp when it comes to having faith. I'm a wimp when it comes to praying too. I'm certainly not one of those prayer warriors I've heard about. I'm more of a prayer *worrier*!

So I admit it. I'm a puny wimp when it comes to faith. A wimp when it comes to prayer. In fact, I'm a wimp when it comes to life. Maybe I should have called this book *Confessions of a Prayer, Faith, Life, and Everything Else Wimp*!

I'm no theologian. I'm no Bible scholar. I've never been to seminary or Bible college. I have never written a Bible thesis or done an exhaustive exegesis (whatever that is) on anything. I never even went to Sunday school as a kid.

I have read the Bible, and even manage to remember parts of it after I close the cover, but I'm certainly no expert. I am mystified why the whole thing couldn't have been put in chronological order. Wouldn't that make it a little easier to follow?

And I can't keep all those Bible guys straight. There are Joshua, Jehoshaphat, Jeremiah, and Job. Jedediah, Josiah, Jesse, and James. Then there are Jaazaniah, Jacob, Jonathan, and Joel. Let's not forget John, John, and John Mark. And Judas and another Judas, along with Judah, Jehu, Jotham, Joseph, Jonah, Jezreel, Jeroboam, and . . . well, you get the picture. No wonder I get confused.

Enough about who I am not. Here's who I am: I am a woman, a wife, and a mother. I'm a stepmother, grandmother, daughter, sister, and friend. I take care of a home. I hold down a job. I write. I speak. I laugh. I cry. Sometimes all at the same time. (Especially lately. If you're a woman over forty, you know what I'm talking about.)

I try to take care of myself, watch my weight, eat right, get enough sleep, and drink enough water. I exercise, sort of. I get regular medical checkups. I get my teeth cleaned twice a year, and between visits I floss. At least for the first week after a cleaning and the last week before the next one.

I'm just an average woman. An average woman trying to figure out what it means to live life, to have faith. I have a lot of questions about life and faith, and I've included some of those questions at the end of each chapter. Use the questions by yourself for pondering or for journaling. Use them with a friend, in your book club, or in a church group. Use them or

ignore them. It's entirely up to you. Thinking is always
optional.

I'm just an average woman trying to figure out how everything—life, grief, family, joy, God, and cellulite—how it all
fits together. I'm just a woman fumbling my way through the
clutter, confusion, and sometimes chaos of life. Trying to get
my act together. Trying to find the strength for my struggles.
Trying to find my way home.

Maybe you're trying to find your way too. Maybe we can
do it together.

> Those who know your name will trust in you,
>   for you, LORD, have never forsaken those who seek you.
> —Psalm 9:10

getting my
act together

part one

thank God for pine-sol!

Part of my problem—maybe most of my problem—in trying to find my way and trying to figure things out has been this: I'm not a very organized person. I am not neat by nature. I wasn't born organized like so many other women I know. My more organized friends, especially the spreadsheet-loving math majors and accountants among them, tend to think in neat rows and columns. It's easy for them to stick to schedules, establish boundaries, and keep things orderly and functioning smoothly. They're naturals.

I'm not a rows-and-columns type. I tend to think in wide-open spaces (I seem to have so much right there between my ears) and in blobs and splashes of bright color. Don't misunderstand. I love making plans and setting goals. I love setting up organizational systems, especially when they involve flashy colored file folders, brightly decorated boxes, and gorgeous baskets. I love setting up a new plan or a new system. I just hate sticking with it for very long. New is exciting. Old is boring. I have to move on.

I am not neat by nature. It's been a struggle since child-hood to get my act together. And to keep it that way. My mother—sorry, Mom—didn't help much. She cleaned our apartment on Fridays while I was at school or out playing. The finer details of the cleaning process, the how-tos of home maintenance, remained a mystery, but I grew up intimately familiar with the smell of "Pine-Sol clean." To this day, if I get just a whiff of Pine-Sol, I think, *It must be clean!* I confess that sometimes I skip cleaning altogether and just swish a little Pine-Sol around the sinks and countertops. Then, as company is ringing the doorbell, I twirl the Pine-Sol–drenched rag above my head a few times before I open the door. Fools 'em every time.

My friends have helped me over the years, mostly my blobs-and-splashes friends who have shared their own house-hold hints for the cleaning-impaired: "Spray the front door with lemon-scented Pledge. Anyone who comes to the door will assume you've been cleaning." This variation on the Pine-Sol plan works great.

Another friend said, "Just keep the vacuum cleaner parked in the living room. Everyone will think they caught you in the middle of your chores." This worked for a while, but then I had trouble explaining the cobwebs growing from the vac-uum. Speaking of cobwebs, one friend swears she heard one of those decorating divas on TV suggest that instead of fret-ting over cobwebs, you should just spray them with gold paint at Christmas and make them part of your holiday decor. Keen idea.

My friends have been helpful, but for years my house-cleaning mentor was Phyllis Diller, who claimed the only thing domestic about her was that she was born in the United States. Her advice? You never have to clean at all if you just keep your bathrobe and a stack of get-well cards handy. When unexpected company shows up, throw on the robe, scatter the cards around, and open the door sniffling, "Pardon the mess. I'm just getting over the flu." (You have to practice a little to get the right raspy, pathetic sound in your voice, but it's worth the effort.)

Since I was not born organized, my childhood bedroom was a disaster area. Every couple of months, I'd hear my mother faintly calling encouragement to clean things up. At least I think it was my mother. I couldn't really see her from behind my piles of stuff.

My piles of stuff grew as I lived at home during college. I had several years' worth of *Time* and other magazines stacked in my room. "I'm saving them for when I become a teacher," I said during my freshman year. (Did I honestly expect my future second graders to read *Time*?) I used the same excuse in my sophomore and junior years as boxes full of fabric and yarn scraps for future art projects filled every available spot in the house.

One day in my senior year of college, my mother let out a holler from the direction of the back hall utility closet. I found her buried under an avalanche of empty shoeboxes (for the Valentine's Day "post office" we'd build in my classroom), old newspapers (for future papier-mâché projects), and a hundred or so empty egg cartons (for my future students' Mother's Day tulips, of course).

"What's going on here? I'm living with Fibber McGee!" she yelled from under the rubble. (She loved that old radio show with the crazy guy with the overflowing closet. I was sorry I hadn't been around to hear it. I might have picked up some household hints.)

"Creative minds are rarely tidy?" It sounded like a lame excuse even to me, but it was the best I could come up with on such short notice. After college I left my stuff behind to live out of state temporarily. While I was gone, my mother moved to a different house. To this day, she insists the timing was sheer coincidence. In the move, my stuff was "somehow" lost. Another coincidence, she says. Who knows how many of my second graders missed achieving their full creative potential for want of an egg carton or a copy of *Time* from 1962.

I vowed to get organized once I had children of my own. Children came. Messiness increased. I now had several people's piles to deal with. "Once they're all potty trained" became "once they're all in school." Meanwhile, I continued to take action only when the piles became overwhelming or when the family was desperate for clean clothes.

One morning I found my sweet husband, Terry, singing in front of our nearly empty closet, "Oh, where, oh, where has my clean clothing gone?"

"Oh, look, oh, look in the dryer," I sang back, proud that I had recently done laundry. He went to the laundry room and came back looking bewildered, carrying the rumpled lump of crinkled cotton that had been his shirts. I blushed, knowing three days in the dryer had done the damage.

I tried to shift the blame. "Ha! They have the nerve to call these 'permanent press'!" I said, grabbing the shirts and heading out to see if I could unearth the ironing board.

I knew I had to change my ways. My hardworking man (aka Saint Terrance, the Patron Saint of Long-suffering Husbands) deserved better. I had promised myself I'd get organized once the kids were in school. My oldest was starting to shave. I was out of excuses. I was the homemaker after all. It was time I made a home.

Things changed when I found a book written by two sisters, self-proclaimed slobs like me. They assured me I wasn't hopelessly disorganized. I was simply, as their title said, a Sidetracked Home Executive. Their index-card file system was designed for people like me—people with untidy creative minds. People who might be able to keep their ducks in a row if they could just find their ducks. People who love setting up new systems.

And what a system they had. It appealed to me on every possible level. It involved purchasing supplies. I loved that. It involved index cards in various colors—white, blue, yellow, green, and my favorite, pink. I loved that. It required a numeric 1-to-31 index, a January-to-December index, and an A-to-Z index. I loved that. It needed a gorgeous three-by-five-inch file box—in the color and design of my choice! Oh, what fun I had shopping and setting it all up!

The sisters suggested writing each task on a three-by-five card, the color depending on the frequency of the task. One color for daily chores, another for weekly chores, and so on. What fun! Thanks to the sisters' system, I began to make progress, little by little. And I learned to delegate. The whole family got involved. I started to like this new, organized way of life. At last I'd found a system that could work for me over the long haul—in other words, more than a week. What a heady feeling.

You've probably realized by now that I'm an all-or-nothing kind of gal. Before long I was hooked on getting organized. I'd discovered a new and fascinating area of study. I started collecting organization books. Dozens of them. I became obsessed with the tools of the organized life. I bought files, caddies, holders, and trays for my office. I hauled home bathroom organizers and garage systems.

In my kitchen, I alphabetized my spices. I established a baking center, a cooking center, and a table-setting center. I designated and labeled the kitchen utensil drawers by frequency of use: the FUU drawer for Frequently Used Utensils, the LFUU for Less Frequently Used Utensils, and the SUU drawer for Seldomly Used Utensils. Heaven help the kitchen helper who didn't know which utensils belonged where!

I had gone from organizational misery to organizational mania. I was addicted to order. My family worried where it would all end. When I began referring to my children by their chores and responsibilities—Cat Box Boy, Dishwasher Girl, and Garbage Can Baby—the family staged an intervention. They cornered me one night in the family room.

Cat Box Boy let me have it. "I am *not* just a 'pooper scooper'! I am a human being!"

Dishwasher Girl informed me, "We are *more* than our *chores*!"

And Garbage Can Baby cried, "Mommy! Don't call me that!"

Even Terry said I was driving him crazy cleaning up after him. "Can't you just relax a little, honey? I think you're going just a tad overboard with this whole thing ... Hey, I wasn't done wearing those shoes! Put them back on my feet!"

They were right. I'd gone way too far. I'd come to love the daily fix that being organized gave me. I had gotten to the point where I didn't care what was going on in my life, in my head, or in my heart as long as the house was neat and clean. That's all that seemed to matter.

But more mattered. My family's feelings mattered. My own feelings mattered. What God thought mattered. It was time to stop the madness. I realized I'd been wearing myself out trying to get my act together. I realized that God had something different in mind, something that saner people might call "balance."

I found the balance I needed in Luke 10:38–42, where Jesus spends time with two sisters. Sister Mary seems to be like me—a blobs-and-splashes kind of woman. The other, Martha, seems to be a bit more of the rows-and-columns type. Jesus tells the organized one, "You are worried and upset about many things, but only one thing is needed."

Only one thing. I started to get the message. Spending time with God was what really mattered. Maybe if I let him clean up my life from the inside out first, the rest of my stuff would fall into place. Maybe.

I want to be organized, but I don't want the nagging of my to-do list to drown out his voice inviting me to sit at his feet and learn from him. "Come to me," he says, "all you who are weary and burdened, and I will give you rest" (Matthew 11:28).

I hear that invitation even a little more personally: "Come to me, all you harassed and harried, all you confused and cluttered, all you running and ragged, all you messy and meandering. Take a load off. Put your feet up."

I want to be organized, not as an end in itself, but to give me time for the really important things in life. There is a system, I'm learning, that keeps things in better balance and keeps life orderly "enough." A system that puts first things first. A system that allows time for doing what God put me here to do and allows plenty of time for what really matters. Time for hugging. Time for celebrating the love of God, family, and friends. Time for laughing.

I laughed the other day, realizing that as organized as I'm learning to be, no system is foolproof. My friend Kathy, the church librarian, sent me an overdue notice from the church library. She added a personal note: "You checked this book out six months ago. Do you still have it, or is it lost?" I didn't have a clue.

The name of the overdue book? It was the sidetracked sisters' sequel: *Get Your Act Together*!

> Seek first his kingdom and his righteousness, and all these things will be given to you as well.
>
> —Matthew 6:33

points to ponder

1. Are you more of a rows-and-columns woman or a blobs-and-splashes gal? Explain. How has your personal style helped or hindered your ability to keep your life on track?

2. How do you stay organized? What works for you? What needs changing?

3. "Only one thing is needed," Jesus said. How do you think your life would change if you focused on the one thing Jesus says we need? What other "needed" things keep you from doing that?

little house — unplugged

We just bought a new stove to replace the old harvest-gold warhorse that had served our family through two decades of macaroni and cheese and frozen pizza. This stove is all digital, with at least as many features as the space shuttle. The manual reads like rocket science, but I doubt even a NASA engineer could figure it all out.

It took me a while to figure out how to set the clock. The clock? How complicated can a clock be? Incredibly complicated, it turns out. "Hold down the left button while depressing the right button advancing by five-minute increments. Release when time is set." Buttons? Increments? What happened to hands, dials, and knobs? I don't have the eye-hand coordination for all that holding and releasing. I blew past the correct time and had to start all over again. And again. Holding and releasing. Releasing and depressing. It was depressing all right.

The new stove has no burners (those circular heating devices that have always been so aptly named at our house). These are "cooktop cartridge heating elements" completely sealed in smooth black ceramic. You can't tell there are electrical elements inside until you see the deep-red glow as they heat up. They glow like the inside of a volcano. Blackened pancakes, anyone?

I can toss out the rubber gloves and the Easy-Off spray. This new oven cleans itself, somehow. I haven't dared to try it. The manual cautions, "WARNING! Internal temperatures may exceed 1,000 degrees." I don't want to risk that. Since the old cleaners will damage the oven surface (another WARNING!), I guess I'm stuck with a dirty oven. At least until a firefighter moves in next door.

The "time-bake" feature promises to give me convenience and freedom. All I need to do is set the clock (ha!), pick a temperature (from 1 to 1,000 degrees), and walk away. What good does that do me? I still have to shop for the ingredients, don't I? I still have to assemble them, right? I still have to put it all in the oven, don't I? All this marvelous feature has done is add another step—a very complicated step—to an already tedious process.

I can see it all now. I go through the process to get it all set up and leave the house. While I'm gone, my chicken-enchilada casserole bakes for seven and a half hours at 1,000 degrees. I arrive home to find the fire department wetting down the last of the embers. I'm crushed. My chicken enchiladas won't be winning any bake-offs as "Chicken Incinerata"!

The technological advances that were supposed to make life easier have just made everything so much more complex. Psychologists call it the paradox of progress. So many technological advances in the past century! And 99 percent of those have made their way into our house in the past decade.

Have they made life easier? Absolutely not. More stuff to dust, upgrade, insure, and store. More manuals to study, more systems to master, more things to go haywire. How did we get ourselves into this? I blame Terry. He's a techno-junkie.

I've seen him drooling over the Sunday paper's advertisements from stores like Land O'Tech and Comput-A-Rama. He dreams of standing in line with a hundred other eager suckers—oops! I mean shoppers—queuing up at dawn the morning after Thanksgiving (that most hallowed of shopping days). Waiting for the store to open at 7:00 a.m., each shopper hopes to be the lucky one to score the EARLY BIRD SPECIAL! ONLY ONE PER STORE! NO RAIN CHECKS! (Do the math, people!)

Terry's hooked on technology. I've seen him shaking, suffering withdrawals when the hard drive crashed on his home-office computer. I've seen him focused like a laser on fixing it. Hours—days!—passed before he surfaced, and that was only to ask me to help him find his teeny-tiny screwdriver. He'd dropped it somewhere among the dirty dishes and empty soda cans in the room.

Terry loves technology. If it beeps, buzzes, lights up, or calculates, he wants it. So it's no wonder we ended up with a high-tech stove as well as every other electronic gizmo and gadget that's hit the market. But we didn't realize just how wired we were until the house was struck by lightning.

Early one summer morning, around 3:15 a.m., we were awakened by a huge boom of thunder. Loud enough that the whole house shook. Loud enough to wake our little fox terrier, Izzy, from her snooze on the chair in the bedroom. The boom was followed by a brilliant flash of light and another boom. This second boom was loud enough to send poor Izzy flying off the chair and down the stairs to the safety of "her room" off the kitchen. Loud enough that she left a trail of doggy-doo in her wake, across the bedroom floor and down the stairs. That last boom was *loud*.

The house reverberated a moment, and then all was still. (One of those moments of silence that seems much quieter because of the racket that preceded it. Like the silence you hear when the baby finally stops crying.) We got out of bed to investigate. Everything on the main floor seemed fine. The lights still worked. As we neared the basement stairs, we picked up a faint scent of smoke. We ran down the steps to the basement family room.

The mirror on the family-room wall was missing a six-inch crescent from its right edge. The piece was on the floor. On the wall where the piece had been was a nail-sized hole surrounded by a dark circle, like a gunpowder burn. A nail had shot out of the wall stud, through the dry wall, and out through the mirror, breaking the crescent-shaped piece of mirror off cleanly. The nail itself was nowhere to be seen. Pulverized perhaps. Maybe melted.

Lightning had struck. It seemed incredible that lightning would damage this mirror, for the wall on which it hung was a foundation wall in our basement. The wall was completely underground!

Outside the next morning, I found a hole in the ground, a foot wide and just as deep, at the base of an oak tree on the other side of the driveway. A metal driveway marker had been in that spot. Bits of the marker's blue plastic reflector were scattered like shrapnel across the driveway.

The bark on the oak tree was split in several places. We guessed that the lightning had traveled under the driveway, following tree roots maybe, and made contact with the nail behind the mirror. It seemed bizarre, but it was the best theory we had.

Inside the house, the damage was much more extensive than just the broken mirror. The power surge had fried almost all things electronic. We realized that morning how very wired we'd become.

The VCRs (not one, but three!) were no longer blinking 12:00. (Oh, you have one of those too?) The phone lines were dead, melted together at the junction box on the back of the house. The phones themselves—count 'em, six—had to be replaced. The only survivor was an "old-fashioned" phone. Hmm.

Satellite TV was gone; its receiver, switches, and wires were scorched and shorted out. The TV antenna that brings us our local stations was inoperable. Its motor had melted. Televisions—not one, not two, but *three*—were ruined. The furnace fan and the oven vent fan on the new stove needed repair.

The electric water heater survived. Lightning is like a mini-tornado, skipping through the house, devastating some areas, leaving others untouched. Some electrical outlets blew; others were fine. The computers survived—surge protectors work!—but they needed careful attention to restore and safeguard all our data. And all the printers and modems, as well as the fax machine in my office, were shot.

Boy, we had a lot of stuff! Stuff, stuff, and more stuff! We didn't realize how much we had until we had to replace it all at once. As we replaced things, we thanked God we didn't have worse damage. No fire had started. No one had been hurt. We also thanked our insurance company.

In the process of assessing the damage and replacing things, we couldn't help but wonder: Why do we have all this stuff? Do we really need it? How wired, how "connected," are we required to be?

We spent several days without a telephone or an answering machine. An eerie quiet descended upon the house. Nothing

was ringing, beeping, chiming, or chirping. The modems blown,
we spent several days without email. A peaceful calm came over
us. What was this foreign feeling? Leisure? Yes, leisure. We
slowed down. No rushing to the computer, no rushing through
dinner to get to the television. No interruptions to answer phone
calls. No frenzy, no noise. Just time and quiet. I read three books
in four days. I took baths.

Terry and I talked—real conversations. Long conversations. We were unplugged. Ma and Pa Ingalls in our own little house on the prairie, living a suddenly simpler life. Life
before faxes and email. Before twenty-four-hour access to the
world via the Internet. Before the demands of instant acces-
sibility. Peaceful. Quiet.

The quiet didn't last long. A week after our encounter with
the bolt from the blue, we were right back in the technological groove. The phones restored, a friend called and
demanded, "Where have you *been*? I've been trying to *call*
you!" as if I had been on the lam hiding from the feds.

I apologized—*apologized!*—for not being reachable. Why?
Where is it written that we have to be available twenty-four
hours a day, seven days a week, to everyone and anyone who
wants to reach us?

Within the first few hours of having our phones restored,
we had seven unsolicited phone calls. Oh, how I'd missed the
telemarketers. I was so grateful to have them draw my attention once again to the latest credit card deals, the best long-
distance savings plan, and the new and improved enzyme
product guaranteed to keep my septic system running
smoothly for years to come. (Worrying about my septic system often keeps me awake at night.)

Ah, technology. What would we do without it? What
would we do without email? What would our world be like

without cells and pagers, beepers and buzzers, faxes and FedEx? How would we function without overnight delivery, instant messaging, videoconferencing, and webcam live updates? Where would we be without the world at our fingertips and ourselves available at all times, always on call, always moving ahead on the superhighway of progress?

What would we do without technology? I can think of a few things.

> Breathe, sleep, eat, drink, relax.
> Stretch, walk, run, skip, dance.
> Notice, sense, feel, listen, hear.
> Read, write, think, discuss, ponder.
> Pray, praise, worship, adore, thank.
> Laugh. Love. Live.

When was the last time you enjoyed peace and quiet? When was the last time you were unplugged? When was the last time you were quiet enough to hear God speaking?

Don't wait for lightning to strike. Unplug yourself for a while today. You'll be glad you did.

> "I would hurry to my place of shelter,
> far from the tempest and storm."
>
> —Psalm 55:8

points to ponder

1. How has technology changed your life in the past ten years? What's been the positive impact? What's the downside for you?

2. Close your eyes. What do you hear? (Appliances humming, TV, radio, computer noises, traffic?) When was the last time you were quiet enough to hear God? Take some time—maybe right now—to be quiet.

3. If you're brave enough, try unplugging for a week: no television, no computer games, no Internet, no email, no radio, and no CD player. (No phone?) Can you do it? What do you notice? (If you are already unplugged from all of the above, try going without *reading anything* for one whole week. What do you notice?)

clearing the clutter

I want more unplugged moments like this. I sit looking out the kitchen window on this winter morning. The sun, still low in the sky at this time of year, streaks through bare oak limbs, diffused by the branches into a dozen white fingers of light, sparkling through the frost on the window. (I know, I know. Frost is a sign of a poorly insulated window, but it is beautiful nonetheless.) The sun warms my face. It feels so good to just sit like this, staring out the window, quietly doing nothing. I want more of this. I want a simpler life.

I watched a television documentary a while back that showed how tribal women in Kenya spent hours every week gathering firewood and many more hours cooking over open fires. Many hours of work every week just to eat. Then some genius from Harvard showed them the "solar oven." This simple invention reflects heat from the sun through a glass panel into a wooden box. Food cooks inside the box. Time spent gathering wood and cooking is drastically reduced. The women put their food in the box, walk away, and return in a few hours to a fully cooked meal.

Wow! I thought. *It's a Crock-Pot!* But then I wondered, now that they have their first "modern convenience," how long will it be before the tribal women of Kenya wonder what happened to their free time? How long before every spare moment is packed with action and obligation? Before long, they'll need time planners and pagers to manage their busy schedules. And before long, modern living will have them running to the doctor for ulcer medication and signing up for stress-management workshops.

Tribal women of Kenya, welcome to my world!

The life of those Kenyan women is *not* a simple life. Going "back to the soil" and struggling to survive holds no appeal for me. But neither does barely surviving life on the twenty-first-century fast track. There's plenty of room to live a simpler life between those extremes, isn't there?

When son Alex, then twenty, announced he was going to simplify his life, I thought with a laugh, *Oh, that's a great idea, son! Let's see . . . you live in our basement, eat our food, and use our utilities. You're on our insurance policies, you're only working part-time while attending school, and you pretty much come and go as you please. Just how complicated can your life be?*

But then he bought an old car, one he could repair himself, ignoring the pressure to own a newer, status-symbol vehicle, and he paid cash for it. *No car payments? Good idea, son!* Then he cleaned out his stuff, reducing a storeroomful of boxes to a manageable few. He gave a bunch of stuff away and threw away even more. I felt a pang watching his old Cub Scout uniform leave the house (he was so *cute* in that little blue shirt), but I thought, *Less junk to worry about? Less stuff to clean and organize? Good idea, son!*

Where can you find the simple life? Here are a few tricks I've picked up from my rows-and-columns girlfriends. Start in your closet. Create some empty spots in there. Get rid of half your clothes. (*What? Did she really say that?* Yes, I did. Get rid of half your clothes.) Chances are you regularly wear only about 20 percent of the clothes that are stuffed in your closet. Keep only what fits great, looks great, and makes you feel great. Pass the rest along to someone who will wear them. Don't add anything new to your closet without getting rid of something old. (Why are you adding more unless you have something you need to replace?)

Create some space in your cupboards, pantry, and storage areas. Okay, I don't know if you heard the news, but the Great Depression is over. Long over. Are you a hoarder? I used to be, until the day I added up the money that was sitting on my storage shelves in the form of extra cans of cream of mushroom soup (the secret ingredient in a thousand recipes I make), backup mayonnaise, and rolls of toilet paper. I was preparing for Y3K, I guess.

I let go of the fear that said I needed to have all this *just in case* of a flood; we live on top of a big hill, and from what I can tell, that Noah thing was a onetime deal. *Just in case* of an earthquake, though we live in a no-fault zone. *Just in case* of a nuclear holocaust; but really now, will an extra case of toilet paper matter if that happens?

I decided to take the money I had tied up in all that inventory and put it to work in the savings account instead. I can use the cash to restock the cream of mushroom supply when I run out. In the year 2045. Now that's what I call emergency preparedness.

Create some clean spaces in your home. Keep only what you deem useful, beautiful, or uplifting. I give you permission to toss out that ugly lamp you've always hated, the one Aunt Edwina gave you as a housewarming gift. Pass it on to someone who can appreciate it. One woman's "disgusting" is another woman's "divine." Every decorating diva knows that.

Thomas à Kempis wrote, in *Of the Imitation of Christ*, "Endeavor therefore to withdraw your heart from the love of visible things, and to turn yourself to things invisible." It is so easy these days to feel the pull of visible things, isn't it?

A doctor friend of ours returned from a medical mission trip to South America. He had seen for the first time how people in other countries live. He came home to his large (by middle-class American standards) home on several acres in the country, where he and his wife lived with their three children. "We realized we were way 'overhoused,' that we had enough room for several families," he said.

He and his wife, after much prayer and discussion, decided to downsize their living quarters and simplify their lives. They decided to unplug the consumption machine. They put their big house with all its acres on the market and found a significantly smaller house. They divested themselves of all kinds of gadgets and gizmos, cancelled the cable, and eliminated the extras. The lowered living expense enables them to give more generously to help others.

God is giving them great joy in their decision to withdraw themselves from the "love of visible things." They're redefining themselves as children of God instead of consumers of the world.

Create some space in your workplace. I was appalled when I cleaned out my desk on the last day at a job. I could not believe all the things I was storing, just in case. My desk was a repository of corporate history—outdated manuals for equipment that had long since died, instructions for systems we were no longer using, and hard copies of emails from employees who were no longer with the company. What a pile of junk! What was I keeping it for?

"Just in case" was the rationale. Just in case what? Just in case we ever bought more dial phones? Just in case we needed to know who was head of accounting in 1965? Just in case we went back to the "old" system? That was the "system that worked so well I still don't know why we switched" system. You know the one I'm talking about, don't you? That was four systems ago.

The stuff I'd stashed was worthless. It wasn't giving me any job security. It's not like I had pictures of the boss doing something illegal. I can't tell you why I kept it all, but getting rid of it felt wonderful. Don't wait until your last day. Give yourself the delight of divesting. Dump the junk!

Speaking of clearing the clutter, lose the attitudes that complicate your life. Get rid of "stinkin' thinkin'"—the mental clutter that keeps you from doing what you want to do, from living the life God wants you to live. A life in which you experience the joy of operating out of the center of your giftedness. A life in which all the pieces of your puzzle come together. A life of fulfillment, contentment, and peace.

What's your excuse? "I'd like to do that, but I'm too ..." What? Are you too old or too young? Are you too fat or too poor? Too rich or too thin? (Can we be?) Too short or too tall? Are you too underqualified or too overqualified? Are you too late? Are you just too scared?

We limit ourselves with thoughts that somehow there is a right age, a magic weight, a proper background, or a perfect time. Check with God on that. I believe you'll discover that he has a plan for you for right now, right here. He can use you just as you are. Don't wait. Start now. Lose that limitation thinking. With God, all things are possible.

Get a new perspective. I whine about shopping—the lines, the crowds, the hassle. Then I remember a friend writing from overseas about a three-hour wait to buy groceries in a store that was confusing, understocked, and overpriced. She had to transfer four times on unreliable public transportation to get there. Perspective.

When they were young, my children, boisterous and clamoring for attention, interfered with my plans at times. "A little peace and quiet, please!" I'd holler. Then I'd remember a friend whose child was chronically ill, with only enough energy to be quiet. Perspective.

My husband leaves his dirty socks on the floor, sometimes within inches of the clothes hamper. I pick them up, grumbling. Then I remember how he looked when they wheeled him out of the heart surgery that saved his life. I remember what a gift we've been given—another day, a second chance. Perspective.

Complaining complicates life and strips the joy from living. Perspective helps.

Clear some space in your schedule, some time to do nothing. Some time to just think. Life is simpler when you know your purpose. Why are you here? A friend says it doesn't matter why we are here or what we do, because a hundred years from now, nobody is going to know the difference. What do you think?

Decades ago Robert Frost wrote his poem "Stopping by Woods on a Snowy Evening." Reading it today, I am moved by his words, by the picture of the man and his horse, stopping in dark, wintry stillness to "watch the woods fill up with snow." He longs to stay there but remembers that he has "promises to keep and miles to go before I sleep." Just like me. Frost's decision to stop and watch the snow, and to write about it, matters to me today. My pessimistic friend is wrong. Almost a hundred years later, Frost makes a difference.

I want a simple life with uncluttered space to put the most important things first in my schedule. I want to wake up thankful for life and breath and health. I want less confusion and more calm, less stress and more sanity. Each day is a gift, a fresh chance to love people. I want the time, the space, and the energy to do that.

I want more time to watch the woods.

Looking out the kitchen window on this wintry morning, I savor the last few moments of my break. The sun is higher, brighter now. I squint at it, and the sunlight dissolves into a hundred little rainbows. Such a simple thing, this dollop of sunshine on my face. Such a splendid thing, to sit and do nothing. Where is the simple life? In moments like these.

In another moment, I know, I'll have to get back to those promises I have to keep and the miles I must cover before I sleep. But for this moment, I close my eyes, feeling God's presence and peace, thinking about how a hundred years from now, what I do today might be making a difference in someone's life, somewhere out there in time.

But for now, I sit and smile. This is my moment in the sun.

Now this is what the LORD Almighty says: "Give careful thought to your ways."

—Haggai 1:5

points to ponder

1. Where is the clutter in your house? What kind of mental clutter are you hanging on to? How can you let it all go? How can you have a simpler life?

2. What is the biggest drain on your time and energy? Ask yourself, "How can I improve this situation?" and list ten possible alternatives. (Don't think too hard. Just list ideas as they come to mind. Ask a close friend for additional ideas.)

3. Sometime today take a walk outdoors or sit quietly in a cozy spot and "give careful thought to your ways," as the Bible says. Think about the sources of clutter and confusion you have identified in your life. Then ponder the peace you find in God's presence. Ponder your many blessings as well and give thanks.

hand over the metal bra
and nobody gets hurt

The motivational speaker commanded, "Repeat after me:
No. No! *No!*"

We, her female audience, obeyed. "No. No! *No-o-o!*" We
really belted out that last one.

The speaker explained, "I just wanted you to have that
experience. Some of you have never said that word before!"

Judging from the number of faces turning red, she was
right.

Why is it so hard for us to just say no? Will you bake the
cookies for the school party? Sure. Will you pick up the scout
troop after the carnival? Yup. Can you address the invitations
and decorate the reception hall? No problem. Can you run the
errands, clean the house, work the full-time job, smile, have
dinner ready on time, do all the laundry, lead the pack, and
deliver the doughnuts? You betcha!

We are woman. Hear us roar.

I was invited to speak to a professional organization. It
was a lucrative offer, but the timing was wrong. I had writing
deadlines and a family member was sick. The presentation

would take several days to prepare, and traveling to and from the event would be exhausting. I would need time afterward to recover from the energy drain.

All these were great reasons to decline the invitation, but still I struggled to "just say no." Why was it so hard? Because I wished I could find some way not to disappoint the people inviting me to speak, not to disappoint my editor by missing my deadline, and yet remain available and flexible to meet my family's needs. I agonized for days—days!—over my answer. I wished I could be in two—or three—places at once. I wished I could be two—or three—people at once. I wished I could be Wonder Woman. But maybe without the metal bra.

Why is it so hard for us to say such a little word? No. So few letters, so much power.

Moses had to learn to just say no. He was leading the Israelites, acting as mediator for all of their disputes. I can't imagine how he did it. I had trouble enough getting the kids to stop squabbling. I finally resorted to hollering, "If you disturb the parents, you are *all* grounded!" That at least taught them to squabble quietly. But getting back to Moses . . .

Moses got some good advice from his father-in-law, Jethro. "When his father-in-law saw all that Moses was doing for the people, he said, 'What is this you are doing for the people? Why do you alone sit as judge, while all these people stand around you from morning till evening?'

"Moses answered him, 'Because the people come to me to seek God's will. Whenever they have a dispute, it is brought to me, and I decide between the parties and inform them of God's decrees and laws.'"

Doesn't that sound good, like Moses was doing a wonderful thing, helping the people? Jethro didn't think so. "Moses' father-in-law replied, 'What you are doing is not good. You and these people who come to you will only wear yourselves out. The work is too heavy for you; you cannot handle it alone.'" (You can read all about this in Exodus 18:13–27.)

If you have trouble saying no to demands on your time and energy, let me be your Jethro for a moment. What you are doing is not good. You will only wear yourself out. The work you're taking on is too heavy for you. You can't do it all alone. And you don't have to. Really you don't.

Moses took Jethro's advice, and I hope you'll consider it too. Moses started delegating some of his responsibilities to others. Delegating is a beautiful thing. It's how Cat Box Boy and Dishwasher Girl came to be. Moses assembled a trustworthy team of judges and assigned some of his mediator responsibilities to them. By doing so, Moses freed himself to do the other things God had called him to do.

By saying no to some things, Moses was free to say yes to other things. Saying no will do the same for you.

Jesus also knew the challenge of too many demands. There were times when the crowd was clamoring for Jesus' attention and he went off by himself. He left the crowd. He declined the invitation. He just said no.

The Bible tells us in the gospel of Mark that Jesus, after spending the day teaching in the synagogue, was inundated after sunset with people requesting healing. He healed them, maybe staying up well into the night to take care of the people. The next morning, very early—before dawn, the Bible says—he got up, left the house, and went off by himself to pray. His disciples tracked him down.

"Everyone is looking for you!" they exclaimed.

His reply was not what they expected. Jesus said, "Let us go somewhere else—to the nearby villages—so I can preach there also. That is why I have come" (see Mark 1:32–38).

Fascinating, isn't it? Jesus declined the invitation to be all things to all people at all times. Jesus said no. If he did, why can't we?

Just because people request our time and energy doesn't mean we have to say yes. We can follow Jesus' example and decline the invitation. Does this mean we turn into self-absorbed, self-centered jerks? Did Jesus? I think not!

Why was Jesus able to say no? Because he knew his mission. "That is why I have come," he said. He had the big picture of his life in mind. He evaluated requests for his time and attention in light of that big picture. He came not just to heal, but to preach. Not just to the one group, but to others. "That is why I have come," he said. That is why he could say no.

Why have you come? Why are you here? Do you have a vision for your life? Do you know why God put you on this earth? To be a spouse? A parent? To teach? To manage a business? To write? To dance? To minister? To paint? To compute? To counsel?

Knowing why you are here—your unique mission—gives you a frame through which to view all requests for your time. That will help you say yes confidently to those things *only* you can do and to gracefully decline other invitations. Knowing why you are here will help you find balance.

What is it only you can do? Only you can have your relationship with God. Only you can be the mate to your mate, the parent to your children. Only you can write your stories, paint your pictures. Fill in the blank for yourself.

"Only I can _____."

Let's take a practical example: You get a request to help at your son Johnny's school carnival. How does that request fit in with your big picture? If, in your big picture, you work full time outside the home in addition to your home duties, you will ask, "Is this something *only* I can do?" If not, let somebody else take on the task.

If, in your big picture, you are a full-time homemaker and at-home mother with time and energy for volunteering at your child's school, then you may say yes without hesitation, provided you haven't already agreed to do more than you are humanly capable of doing.

Sometimes the problem is that my big picture is out of focus. I say "Yes!" to the carnival request even though I work full time and come home exhausted every day. Even though I've already given hundreds of woman-hours to Johnny's school. Even though I feel the pressure of work and home projects I've let slide because I felt so guilty about not being available for little Johnny.

I say "Yes!" anyway because my big picture is out of whack. I think that saying yes makes me the Best Mommy in the Whole Wide World. But guess what? Johnny already thought that before I ever baked a cookie or manned a carnival booth. So I'm not really doing it for Johnny, am I?

Why am I doing it, then? Because I want Johnny's teacher and all the other mommies—and maybe even God—to think I am the Best Mommy in the Whole Wide World. That I am Wonder Woman and Betty Crocker rolled into one gorgeous package. And that, my friend, is ego at work. Ego demanding to be fed. Ego getting me in over my head. Ego running my life. Ego ruining my life.

I'm learning, slowly, that I need to evaluate each request carefully. Is guilt pressing me to say yes? (Betty Crocker feeds the world. Why can't I make one little batch of cookies?) Is it ego? Am I feeding my Wonder Woman pride? (Watch it! That bra could poke somebody's eye out!)

Or is this request in line with God's big picture for my life, in sync with my gifts and my purpose here? To give myself time to think about these issues, I'm learning to say, "Let me get back to you on that." It's a step toward learning to say no.

Let me get back to you on that after I've had time to check my calendar. After I've had time to pray about the request. After I've had time to check the family's calendar for conflicts. After I've had time to calculate how long your request will take and to compare that to the number of hours I have available. (Alas, last time I checked, my days still only had twenty-four hours in them!)

Let me get back to you on that after I've compared what you are asking me to do with my real mission in life, with the first call on my time and energy, with what really matters to me. Let me get back to you on that after I've thought, prayed, compared, analyzed, calculated, and talked it over with the important people in my life. After I've figured out how this request will affect my balance.

Let me get back to you on that in three *days*, not three *seconds*.

There are clearly times we need to just say no. Yesterday I had no time to spend with God. No time for praying. No time for reading the Bible. No writing, no journaling, no quiet reflection. No time for thinking. Nothing. Zero. Zip. Zilch.

There was just too much to do and too little time. I was up late the night before at a meeting, so I slept later than usual. I had appointments out of the office in the morning. I had to take Izzy to the groomer and then go and get my own hair cut. A friend wanted to have lunch, and I had several other errands. The day just got away from me.

Was there anything on that list I should have said no to? Were there things that only I could do? Only I could get my hair cut; that's a tough one to delegate. Only I could lunch with my friend; she accepts no substitutes. The rest of the things on my list I could have delegated or rearranged for other days when I had more time available. The bottom line: just saying no to some of those good things would have given me time and energy for the best things.

I'm practicing saying no to things that are not in line with my mission and my goals. Things other people can do, probably better than I can.

I don't like admitting I'm not Wonder Woman. Does it get easier, with practice, to just say no?

Let me get back to you on that.

> Trust in the LORD with all your heart
>> and lean not on your own understanding;
> in all your ways acknowledge him,
>> and he will make your paths straight.
>> —Proverbs 3:5–6

points to ponder

1. Repeat after me (Come on, say it out loud!): "No. No! *No-o-o!*" How did that feel? Do yourself a favor and say *No!* twice this week to new requests for your time and energy. Practice saying "Let me get back to you on that" to *every* request in the next few days. How does it feel?

2. How's your balance these days? When is it hardest for you to "just say no"? Why do you think that is?

3. Why are you here? What has God put you on this earth to do? What are the things that *only* you can do? How can you allow more time and energy for them?

# of mice and hula hoops

I heard a story in second grade about two mouse cousins. One lived in the city and the other lived in the country. The story idealized country living. In America after World War II, suburbs sprawled, gobbling up pastureland and marauding through meadows. The story's author had an obvious fondness for "the good old days." The story wasn't really a children's story. It was anti-industrialization, anti-development propaganda disguised as a children's story.

Country Mouse lived in humble digs, eating simple crusts of bread and scrounging morsels from the farm pantry. His city cousin lived a fast-lane kind of life in opulent (by mouse standards) surroundings. Country Mouse went to visit City Mouse and envied his rich city cousin's lifestyle until the two mice encountered all kinds of dangers—the dark side of city living. Dangers like mousetraps, car tires, and hungry alley cats. Real dangers to little mice and to impressionable second graders.

The stress of city living got to Country Mouse, and he scurried home. The lesson was clear: stay away from the city! We, city kids all, sighed with relief at the end of the story when Country Mouse was safe at home, enjoying the peace and quiet.

I felt just like Country Mouse a few months ago when I was heading back home to my little house in the Wisconsin woods after a trip to southern California. Terry and I and the children had lived in the Los Angeles area for several years. Familiar with the hassle and confusion of Los Angeles Airport (LAX), we avoided flying to and from LAX whenever possible.

So on this particular trip, we arranged to arrive and depart through the Ontario, California, airport—a smaller facility east of Los Angeles. We flew into Ontario and rented a car. For a week, we held our breath as we drove the California freeways to visit our adult children, grandchildren, and old friends.

The morning we were scheduled to return home, we arrived at Ontario, returned the rental, and finally exhaled as the car-rental shuttle dropped us at the terminal. Our relief was short-lived. The ticket agent told us we had to be rerouted through LAX due to mechanical problems with our scheduled flight.

Remember that song about how "it never rains in southern California"? The next line says it all: "It pours ... Man, it pours!" Pour it did that morning. A gigantic storm system had dumped rain over the immense city the previous day and through most of the night. And it continued to pour.

Seven of us were herded into a small van, courtesy of the airlines, and shuttled to LAX, about an hour's drive. The freeway was packed with cars and trucks, five lanes heading west, bumper to bumper through the deluge. Big city mice don't let a little thing like zero visibility slow them down. We wove in and out of the partially flooded carpool lane, left and right, faster and slower, jostling down the freeway like steelies in a pinball game. *Bing, bong, tilt!*

Trying to keep my breakfast where it belonged—in my stomach—I looked out the van window at the acres of cars and concrete and asked myself what I had often asked before: *Who in their right mind chooses to live like this?*

For most of my life, I did. A city mouse for over forty years, I'm familiar with the noise, the crowds, and the frantic herding from one spot to the next. I've sat in gridlock. I've elbowed my way through the masses at airports. I've sensed my insignificance in a sea of people. Who am I in that sea? Just another faceless blob, blending in with a thousand other faceless blobs.

On that day at LAX, I was just another name on the airline's manifest, just another customer buying Dramamine at the airport newsstand. I waited in line at airport security with everyone else, just another body in the mass of humanity shuffling from one place to the next, hoping to be safe, hoping to make it home. Just another person in the crowd, watching the guy with the hula hoops.

This man, in line ahead of me, bound for an overseas flight, carried two hula hoops. He tried to make the hula hoops fit on the conveyor belt that leads into that machine with the opening with the black flaps that look like a car wash. You know the machine I'm talking about? Carry-on luggage fits through that opening. Shoes, jackets, purses, and laptops fit through the opening. Hula hoops, he learned—we all learned—do not fit. It's that round peg, square hole thing.

Oh, but these were no ordinary hula hoops. These were sparkling, bejeweled hula hoops. These were dazzling, iridescent hoops, most likely souvenirs from one of the southern California theme parks. The man took one hoop and set it on the conveyor belt. The hoop slid forward a few inches and stopped. The rubber belt continued to move, but the hoop stuck out on both sides of the opening. The man, evidently not a geometry major in school, picked up the hoop and tried to shove it through the scanner on the diagonal. Still too big.

He then tried to compress the hoop into an oval. The hoop cooperated as long as the man maintained the pressure. As soon as he let it go, however, the hoop sprang back to a full circle. *Sproing!* He tried again. Squish. *Sproing!* And again he squished! His face turned red with the effort. *Sproing!* (I'm guessing what he said then was not a nice thing in his language. Or any other language.)

By now some in the crowd were chuckling. Watching this comedy, I wondered why he was bothering to take hula hoops on the plane. Couldn't he buy hula hoops at home? Could there actually be someplace on this earth where there are no hula hoops? (The mind boggles!) Was there no Wal-Mart, no Super Target in his neighborhood? Was there no Home Shopping Network on his cable TV lineup?

Even if these were special theme-park souvenirs, doesn't everyone have a website these days? Surely a cyber visit to www.sixuniversaldisneyflags@ripoff.com would have been more convenient than this. Was his home beyond the reach of FedEx? Had we made no progress in the last fifty years?

Perhaps these particular hoops were even more special. Perhaps he'd come to America on a quest from his revered father: "Grasshopper, go to America. Bring back something significant, something representative of the Land of Opportunity." The faithful son was returning with the one universal symbol of all-American free enterprise: the sacred hula hoop. Perhaps he planned to donate the hoops to his country's version of the Smithsonian. Generations to come would stand and admire the hoops, oohing and aahing at this amazing invention, this tribute to American know-how.

I snapped out of my reverie when a security guard approached the man. "Sir, you'll have to take your hoops down there," he said, pointing to the far end of the security area. That must have been where the hula-hoop-scrutinizing experts were working that day. I was glad, because the man's determination was making me big-city paranoid. My thoughts turned dark, these being such dark times. Was he a terrorist? A smuggler? What exactly was in those hoops? I prayed the security people would be alert.

The man and his hoops out of sight, I resumed my Country Mouse musings. *Who in their right mind chooses to live like this? Who chooses noise and hassle, crime and paranoia, nerves and neuroses? Don't they realize that not everyone in the world lives this way?*

We arrived back at our small local airport in Wisconsin late that evening, after fourteen hours en route. Our car was in the parking lot, right where we had left it eight days before. Under the streetlight, the only light in the lot. The lot didn't need more than that. It was just one big lot, with no barriers between short- and long-term parking. The long-term people obey the signs telling them to park in the back rows, leaving the front rows for others.

Strolling out to the car, I knew we'd have an orange envelope on our windshield, marked for each of the eight days we'd been parked there. We'd write a check for $32.00 (do the math: four dollars a day to park—incredible!) and mail it in. *Mail it?* Yes. Mail it in. It's the honor system. No metal teeth in the ground, threatening "severe tire damage" to those who try to skirt the law.

All the mice cooperate. That's how it is at Country Airport.

After living away from the city for a decade and a half, I've grown accustomed to country living. Country living is great. But before this turns into anti-industrialization, anti-development propaganda disguised as a grown-up story, let me tell you the truth about country living. It can be just as harried and noisy, just as paranoid and pressured, as city life. In fact, more than once, isolated in my house in the winter while waiting for the snowplow to come, I've thought, *Who in their right mind chooses to live like this?* I've had that same thought when days go by with no contact with the outside world, with nobody but squirrels, chipmunks, and Izzy for company.

I've had that thought when I realize I've spent half my week behind the wheel, driving to and from the city just so we can *do* things. Shuttling the kids back and forth, running errands, and attending meetings. Nothing can be spontaneous; there is no such thing as a "quick trip" from our house.

Life can be hectic—city or country. I've learned that it doesn't really matter if I live in the city or in the country. The problem with my finding peace and balance, the challenge of finding time in the quiet with God, doesn't come with my territory. The problem comes with me. Because as the saying goes, wherever I go, there I am. I'm there, and that's the heart of the problem. It's not my geographic position, but my priorities. It's not my choice of home, but the choices of my heart.

The truth hit me one February morning in a hotel room in Georgetown, just outside Washington, D.C. Terry and I had had several hectic days in the city, taking the Metro in and out of the Capitol area daily to attend a conference and see the sights. On this particular morning, we had no meetings to attend or sights left to see, so I sat in the quiet hotel room writing in my journal.

"Where are you, God?" I wrote. God seemed far away. Thoughts of God had been crowded from my mind by several days spent focusing on the things of this world. I'd been so distracted by the beauty and grandeur, the bustle and noise of the city, I'd not given any thought to God. My Bible sat on the table next to the television, unopened since I'd arrived.

Where are you, God? It seemed to me at that moment that it was so much simpler to see him in the country. In the mountains above Los Angeles, where seasons are marked by changes in the creation, not just by dates on the calendar. In the Wisconsin woods, where I surprised a doe and her fawn one morning. Near a stream in the Rockies, where I heard God's voice in icy water rushing over rocks.

Where are you, God? I stopped writing and opened the hotel drapes. There, right outside the window, was the steeple of the church across the street. On top of the steeple, glinting in the morning sun, was a tall metal cross.

Had it been there all along? Of course. The psalmist wrote, "Where can I go from your Spirit? Where can I flee from your presence? If I go up to the heavens, you are there; if I make my bed in the depths, you are there. If I rise on the wings of the dawn, if I settle on the far side of the sea, even there your hand will guide me, your right hand will hold me fast" (Psalm 139:7–10).

I saw the truth then, that regardless of where I am—city, country, mountains, forest, at home or abroad—God is there. God is everywhere. Omnipresent. In some places, at some times, his presence seems more real to me, but regardless of my perception, the fact remains: God is everywhere, unchanging, all of the time.

I sensed his presence that morning and the rest of the week, in the middle of one of the busiest metropolitan areas of the world. I saw his hand in the beauty of the city, inspiring the architects and the artists whose work I'd been admiring.

I saw him in the markers at Arlington Cemetery. The rows and rows and rows. And rows. I saw him in my own reflection at the Vietnam Memorial wall as I traced my finger over a classmate's name. Gone so long now. Gone so young. Etched there forever. Remembered.

I heard God in the street music, in "What a Friend We Have in Jesus" played on a steel drum for a cupful of spare change. I saw him in the faces of the people—the rich and powerful and the poor and disenfranchised. All created in his image, all sharing something with me: a need for God.

I sensed his peace in the middle of a hectic and harried week because I stopped to pay attention. That's the key. Stopping to pay attention, wherever I am. When I do that, wherever I am, I am home.

Are you here too, Lord, in this room with me? Now?

Yes. "I am with you always, to the very end of the age" (Matthew 28:20).

> The earth is the LORD's, and everything in it,
> the world, and all who live in it.
> —Psalm 24:1

points to ponder

1. Are you a city mouse or a country mouse at heart? How so? Is city or country living better? Why?

2. Where is your heart's "home"? What makes it special to you? (If you like to write, try freewriting, beginning with "My home is . . ." Set the timer for three minutes or more and keep your pen moving, writing whatever comes to mind.)

3. What does it mean that we are God's dwelling place? Under what conditions is it easiest for you to sense God's presence?

lazy Mary, will you get up?

As I confessed earlier, I am not neat by nature. I am also not by nature a morning person. I admire those who wake up fresh and ready to meet whatever the day will bring. One of my friends is like that, waking with a smile on her face and a song on her lips. She loves the local radio station's early morning wake-up routine. An obnoxious rooster crows, followed by a little ditty as irritating as I've ever heard. A far-too-cheery voice sings,

> Good morning, good morning, good morning, it's time to rise and shine!
> Good morning, good morning, good morning, I hope you're feeling fine!
> Come on, get up, get out of bed! Time to get up, you sleepyhead!
> The day is dawning just for you and all your dreams are coming true,
> Doodly doo, doodly doo, doodly doo . . .

I think it's the "doodly doos" that get to me. Nobody should be doodly-dooing that early in the morning. Nobody—*nobody*—should be doodly-dooing before I've had my coffee.

My friend, eager to take on the day, hears that song on her clock radio and leaps out of bed. I don't leap. I groan and roll over when my alarm goes off. I hunker deeper under the covers, reaching one hand out to smack the snooze button— again and again—until I absolutely have to get up.

When my children were old enough to open the refrigerator, I'd set a bowl of dry cereal out on the table at night. I taught them how to open the refrigerator, retrieve the cup of milk I had poured for them, and help themselves to breakfast. When they were a little older, I taught them how to bring Mommy a bowl too.

My toughest morning challenges came when I worked as a stockbroker in California. I had to be at my desk by 6:15 a.m., ready for the market opening at 6:30 a.m. (9:30 a.m. New York time). Ugh.

Saint Terry, who's always been a morning kind of guy, would wake me at five, start the shower, stand me up, hand me my coffee, and push me in the direction of the bathroom. Bless his heart. I'm not sure how I actually drove to my office—half-asleep most days.

After living with Mr. Early Morning Sunshine all these years, I've become more able to function in the early hours. But I've realized that I still need eight to eight and a half hours of sleep a night to function at my best. Therefore, if I'm going to be "early to rise," I also must be "early to bed." My partying days are over. Long, long over.

We need sleep. Good quality sleep is, the experts say, the single most important factor in good health. More important than diet. More important than exercise. More important than heredity.

Lack of quality sleep brings on a myriad of physical problems. Risks of heart disease, stroke, and high blood pressure increase. We are less resistant to illness and more prone to having car accidents. We get clumsier. Problems are harder to solve. We forget stuff when we are sleep deprived. (Where was I? Oh yeah.) Several studies have shown that under-sleeping by just *two hours* a night can have a serious negative impact on our ability to concentrate, solve problems, and think creatively the next day. (If that's true, I've evidently underslept by a couple of decades!)

How much sleep do we need? Some experts say that less than seven and a half hours is not enough for adults. But it seems to be increasingly difficult to get what we need. Blame it on too much electric light. Blame it on too much electronic stimulation—television, videogames, Internet, and email. Blame it on the bombardment of too much information and too many activities. Blame it on jet lag. Whatever the reason, we sleep on average ninety minutes less a night than people did a century ago. That's an hour and a half less sleep. Have our bodies, in the last one hundred years, adapted to require less sleep? I doubt it.

What's the solution? A German inventor recently designed an office desk with a top that converts to a pillow at the push of a button. Why? Because power naps of up to sixty minutes a day (at least four hours before bedtime) supposedly increase productivity.

The applications of this technology intrigue me. Yawning in the slow line at the grocery store? (Is that always the line you pick too?) Just hit a button on the shopping cart and *zip!* the cart converts to a hammock. You snooze until the cashier awakens you with a gentle, "Paper or plastic?" You smile, happy as a mouse in a mozzarella factory. You're relaxed and rested, and you still make it home in time to get the frozen pizza in the oven before the family demands dinner.

Stuck in a traffic jam? Hit a button and the driver's side headrest inflates to cradle your cranium as the seat automatically reclines. Your favorite blanky drops out of the steering column as the brake pedal rises to become your footrest. The car radio tunes itself to a mellow easy-listening station, and you catch forty winks while you're breathing the exhaust.

Feeling a little wilted as you wait in a restaurant for your dinner date? Just lay your purse on the table, hit a button, and *poof!* your purse is a pillow; you're all set for a little presupper siesta. I'm sure Mr. Right won't care if your face is sleep-creased and your forehead reads—backward—"ƎᗡIHWOƆ ƎNIUNƎƓ %00Ɩ."

A good night's sleep. Ahh. What wonders a good night's sleep will do for my disposition. And missing my sleep has an immediate negative affect on my body. When my children were teens and I was working a full-time job with a varying schedule, I rarely managed the minimum seven and a half hours of sleep. Month after month operating on a deficit took its toll.

I went to my doctor—Dr. Jackie—to discuss (okay, I confess; I went to whine) the dozen aches and pains I had begun to experience. Could it be fibromyalgia? Arthritis? Rheumatism? Lyme's disease? Neuritis? Neuralgia? The heartbreak of psoriasis?

"Are you getting enough sleep?" she asked. What kind of question was that? Of course I wasn't getting enough sleep. I ran myself ragged working full time and taking care of the family and the house. A typical schedule for Wonder Woman, I thought.

"Most American women are sleep deprived," Dr. Jackie told me. "We think we have to do it all, be all things to all people. And we're destroying our health." Was it that simple? No exotic disease had afflicted me? I just needed more sleep?

"Can I just get a prescription to fix this?" I asked. That way I could cure what ailed me without taking any time to do it. She shook her head, but she did suggest I try an over-the-counter sleep aid. I tried it. It worked. After a few nights of sleeping solidly for eight or more hours, my hips stopped aching. My legs stopped cramping. My neck and shoulders relaxed. I had more energy.

Sleep. Dr. Jackie was right. The simple answer was the right one.

Why, if sleep is what we know we need, is it so hard for us to allow ourselves to sleep? I know one of my reasons. Throughout my childhood, my mother (sorry again, Mom!) woke me up with a little song: "Lazy Mary, will you get up?" She thought it was a cheerful way to start the day, but I thought otherwise. I knew that lazy was a horrible way to be. And I was Lazy Mary, a stay-in-bed slacker, a good-for-nothing bum who'd sleep her life away.

I know how it's supposed to work—how early to bed, early to rise, makes you healthy, wealthy, and wise. That was easier for Ma and Pa on the prairie, who rose with the sunrise and rested with the sunset. Nowadays, with artificial light and artificial schedules, ours is an on-call 24-7 kind of lifestyle. We have the ability to work, shop, and run at all hours, every day, all year long. And we feel the pressure to do so.

A friend recently realized that she'd been sleep deprived most of her life. She'd felt so ashamed as a child for being a "sleepyhead," all of her adult life she'd forced herself to stay up later than her body dictated. The result? Chronic fatigue, lack of energy, and depression plagued her.

When she started sleeping more, she immediately felt better. Her moods improved, and her strength and energy increased. She had fewer waking hours each week, but so what? She was much happier and far more productive when she *was* awake.

We need sleep. We need rest. It's all part of God's design. How much sleep are you getting? The author of a time-management book suggested working women get up at 4:30 a.m. and keep going until 11:00 p.m. to meet all the demands of family, home, and career. I did the math. That's a mere five and a half hours of sleep a night! I shouted, "You've *got* to be kidding!" at the author and pitched the book into the garbage can.

We need sleep. If you believe the experts, we adults need seven and a half to nine hours a night. (Teenagers need quite a bit more.) While we sleep, the body repairs itself. The brain processes information, forms connections, and draws conclusions. Have you ever solved a problem in your sleep? The brain is an amazing machine.

How many working adults are getting far less than seven and a half hours a night? Sure, there are those individuals who brag that they thrive on four or five hours of sleep, but they are the exceptions. How many of us are functioning day after day, week after week, at a deficit and are suffering physically and mentally for it?

How much sleep do you need? More than you are getting, I'll guess. How can you tell how much sleep you need? Pay attention to your natural rhythms. How much sleep do you get on vacation or on the weekend? When you don't *have* to get up, how long do you sleep? How much sleep does it take for you to feel, honestly feel, rested and refreshed?

When my schedule became flexible, I started sleeping without setting the alarm. That's when I discovered that my minimum nightly sleep requirement was eight to eight and a half hours. I'd been running on much less sleep for years and feeling guilty if I slept "too much."

Now getting "enough" sleep is a top priority for me. I think better, feel better, and function better with enough sleep. I am more patient, more pleasant to be around, and more productive with enough sleep. I laugh more easily, forgive more readily, and love more passionately with enough sleep.

When day is done, my work, my obligations, my responsibilities—the rest of the world—can wait. I need my sleep.

Enough sleep. Ahh. What a great thing! Making the most of my nights allows me to make more of my days. There is so much I want to do in this life, so many things I dream of accomplishing. I don't know how many days I have. God has decided that already, but that's his business. I don't need to know how many there will be; I just need to make the most of each one as it comes along.

How do I do that? Exercising enough to be energized. Focusing enough to be productive. All made possible by getting enough sleep. As I've learned to allow myself adequate sleep, I've become more of a morning person—once I've had my coffee.

Morning, it turns out, is my best time for writing.

Morning is when I'm most friendly, most calm, and most focused.

Morning, it turns out, is when I'm most open to hearing what God has to say, before the details and distractions of the day completely clutter my mind. I'm less frantic in the morning. More willing to sit in expectant silence, listening for his voice, anticipating his touch.

> In the morning, O LORD, you hear my voice;
>   in the morning I lay my requests before you
>   and wait in expectation.
>
> —Psalm 5:3

points to ponder

1. Are you a morning person or a night owl? Have you always been that way? Which is better and why?

2. How much sleep is "enough" sleep? Are you getting enough? Pay attention to your body's signals this week. What steps can you take to ensure proper rest?

3. What rhythm do you sense in your days? What's your "best" (most creative, energetic, awake, alert) time? How can you arrange to spend some of your best time with God this week?

Betty, botox, and beauty

A gorgeous Saturday morning in the spring reminds me of Betty "Princess" Anderson on the old TV show *Father Knows Best*. Teenage Betty, on any given Saturday morning, wore her pedal pushers and her white tailored shirt, usually with the shirttails knotted together at her waist. Her hair under a scarf like her mother's, Betty helped with the household chores and did her hand washables. That's what girls did on Saturday mornings. Saturday afternoons they spent primping for Saturday night, which was always date night. Betty probably washed and set her hair in curlers—brush rollers or sponge rollers, or maybe those little pink rubber alien-pod things known as "spoolies." She might have added a pin curl or two to her bangs. She'd want a spit curl here and there for extra beauty. Betty went through a lot to be beautiful. So do I.

I've lain motionless for half an hour with cucumber slices on my eyes to cool and soothe them. I've slathered mud on my face and waited for it to dry, imagining the mud sucking out all those nasty toxins in my complexion. I smiled at the thought. My face cracked. Not such a good look for me.

I've steamed my pores open over a hot pan of water, inhaling lavender steam for relaxation. I've stuck sticky strips over the bridge of my nose and ripped them off to pull out those nasty pore clogs. I've slammed my pores shut with astringent lotions. I've smoothed gunk on my cheeks to restore my youthful glow. I've dabbed caustic substances under my eyes to shrink puffiness. My poor face.

As for the rest of me, I've waxed and creamed, pumiced and plucked. I've bathed in green tea, oatmeal, chamomile, and vanilla to exfoliate, detoxify, and preserve. I've soaked in warm water scented with peach, jasmine, and rose buds to freshen, sweeten, and soften. I've tried just about every beauty treatment ever touted by a women's magazine, an infomercial, or a state fair huckster. I've bought dermoblasters, epigrinders, chin masters, and lid lifters. And what has it all done for me?

Not a blamed thing. I'm not one iota prettier, but I'm several iotas poorer. What is this mad pursuit of that elusive commodity called "beauty"?

I stopped by to visit a friend the other day at her office. She was upset with her assistant and was trying to unravel a sticky problem. My friend controlled her temper, but her voice was tight, and I could tell her irritation was intense. Here's the weird thing: her face looked completely calm. Judging from her face, she wasn't bothered a bit. I was puzzled until I remembered that she'd told me she'd gotten a Botox injection in her forehead a couple of days before. She might have been mad, but her face hadn't gotten the message. No frown lines, no furrowed brow, in fact, no expression at all. She's hooked on Botox.

She was already upset, so I spared her the latest negative news for Botox junkies. The Botox habit that paralyzes your normal frowning causes the face—which knows better and wants desperately to frown—to use other muscles in order to frown. This causes wrinkles you wouldn't have had otherwise. The saying "There's a new wrinkle" takes on a whole new meaning.

The solution? More money for more Botox injections to paralyze the newly frowning muscles. Oh, to be a dermatologist in this era! I'd get rich quick and retire to a place where nobody cares how I look.

Women have been giving themselves beauty treatments since the beginning of time. I wouldn't be surprised if they uncovered evidence that in the garden, Eve had given herself a nightly avocado-and-mango facial treatment. The Bible's Esther was treated to a whole year of beauty treatments in preparation for meeting the king. Imagine. Six months of soaking in oils and bathing in exotic concoctions. Another six months of perfumes and cosmetics. A whole year in which your full-time occupation is to look, smell, and feel gorgeous. What would that do for you?

What is beauty? Remember the old joke, "Beauty may be skin deep, but ugly goes clear to the bone"? Is there any truth to that? Yes. Deep-down ugly shows. Have you seen the burning eyes of envy, the twisted look of greed, the lecherous leer of lust, or the haughty sneer of judgment? All are ugly looks coming from deep inside.

What of beauty? Is it only skin deep? Certainly physical beauty is only skin deep. Under the skin, physically, we are the same mass of muscle and bone. According to the Bible, beauty isn't skin deep. It's character deep. "Your beauty should not come from outward adornment, such as braided hair and the wearing of gold jewelry and fine clothes. Instead, it should be that of your inner self, the unfading beauty of a gentle and quiet spirit, which is of great worth in God's sight" (1 Peter 3:3–4).

And this from the writer of Proverbs: "Charm is deceptive, and beauty is fleeting; but a woman who fears the LORD is to be praised" (Proverbs 31:30). That's how God defines beauty. The inner character of a woman with a gentle and quiet spirit. The unfading beauty of a life spent in awe of God. Beauty of the spirit is the only kind of beauty that lasts.

Physical beauty doesn't last. It's fleeting. That must be why we always feel we are playing catch-up in the beauty game. Trying to keep our youthful edge, our young appearance. Trying to stay ahead of aging, ahead of our wrinkles. Trying to improve on that reflection in the mirror. What a waste of energy. What a waste of time.

Remember Narcissus? He was that good-looking hunk in classical mythology who broke someone's heart and then was made to fall in love with his own reflection in a pool. He died right there, admiring himself. How often I catch myself staring into my mirror on a good day, admiring how nicely I've pulled myself together. Every moment I spend focused on myself, I'm dead to the rest of the world.

It isn't our own reflection we should be seeking. "One thing I ask of the LORD," the psalmist writes. "This is what I seek: that I may dwell in the house of the LORD all the days of my life, to gaze upon the beauty of the LORD and to seek him in his temple" (Psalm 27:4). The more time we spend gazing at, seeking, and dwelling near to God, the more his character qualities will be reflected in our lives. But that doesn't happen unless we spend *time* with him.

Time with God changes us. Moses proved that. "When Moses came down from Mount Sinai with the two tablets of the Testimony in his hands, he was not aware that his face was radiant because he had spoken with the LORD" (Exodus 34:29). Moses didn't realize his face was radiant, but Aaron and the rest of the crowd saw it. They knew something had happened up there on the mountain. Moses' face was radiant "because he had spoken with the LORD." He glowed after he'd spent time with God. What did that look like? Was he sunburned? Was he gleaming with an otherworldly light? Was he radiating inner peace? What was it in his mountaintop experience that caused the glow?

I attended a women's retreat in the mountains in southern California. I sat one morning next to a mountain stream that flowed clear and sparkling in the early sun. I sat and enjoyed the silence and the early morning peace. A breeze came over the hills carrying the cold, crisp scent of fresh snow and pine needles. I hadn't been home to the Midwest in the winter in six years. I hadn't smelled the combination of pine and snow in all that time.

I inhaled deeply and sensed at once a clear message to my heart. This wasn't just nostalgia for home. God spoke to me clearly during that retreat time, reminding me of who I am, of the person he created me to be. He reminded me that I am his beloved child and that I need him first.

When I returned home, Terry met me on the driveway. "Your face is glowing," he said. I was not surprised. I'd just come from the mountaintop. I had been with God. I was radiant.

What was it in my mountaintop experience that caused the glow? Was it a new sense of God's peace, relaxing my facial muscles? Was it the extra rest? Sleep? Fresh air? Sunshine? Yes, all of those things. But mostly it was time. Time spent talking with God.

We cannot spend time with God and come away the same as when we entered into his presence. In *Celebration of*

Discipline, Richard Foster says of meditation time, "We cannot burn the eternal flame of the inner sanctuary and remain the same, for the Divine Fire will consume everything that is impure." We cannot enter into God's holy presence and remain the same.

When is the last time you got away from it all? Personal retreat time restores the spirit. Not far from here is a retreat center with the ambience of an old monastery. Operated by an order of nuns, the buildings are open for individual or group retreats. The place has a sense of presence. Thick concrete walls and the massive feel of stone exteriors lend a feeling of permanence. Of eternity. There is silence, a deep, deep quiet that quickly permeates the spirit. And there is peace. It's easy to sense the presence of God in a place like that.

As wonderful as a setting like that can be, you don't need a place like that for restoration. What works for you? Perhaps you could benefit from an hour alone at a favorite coffee shop. Maybe you need a whole day away, tucked in a comfy chair in a corner of the library to read, reflect, and pray. Or you might need a night, or a weekend, alone in a hotel for a good night's sleep and some concentrated thinking time to feel you've truly escaped.

How can you make it happen? How can you arrange to have a personal retreat? How can you spend some extended time away from your everyday obligations to allow yourself time to encounter God? God changes us every time we encounter him. Emotional, physical, mental, and spiritual burdens are lifted. We come away radiant.

I've come to relish God's beauty treatments. The dermabrasion of confession. The deep pore cleansing of repentance. I look forward to a good long soak in the Word of God, time to steam my mind open, time to relax in his truth. I love the way the reality of his love seeps into my bones.

It's like a day at the spa with God, being pampered by the truth of his love and care. Spending time with him gives us that certain look, that glow of good spiritual health, and a sense of well-being.

> He turns our frantic fussing into peace.
> He turns our sorrow into acceptance.
> He turns our mourning into dancing.
> He exchanges our shroud of despair
>   for a garment of praise.

In every encounter with the divine, we can't help but be changed. We come away feeling loved and cared for by God Almighty. In every encounter, we will be changed, crowned with beauty. We will be radiant, a reflection of his splendor.

> I sought the LORD, and he answered me;
>   he delivered me from all my fears.
> Those who look to him are radiant;
>   their faces are never covered with shame.
>   —Psalm 34:4–5

points to ponder

1. How do you feel about facials, pedicures, manicures, and massage? What about Botox, chemical peels, dermabrasion, and body wraps? Are they necessary maintenance or selfish indulgence? Defend your position.

2. Have you ever known someone with a "gentle and quiet spirit"? Describe her (or him). What impact did this person have on you?

3. Describe a "mountaintop experience" you've had. What factors made it possible? When could you take a personal retreat? Where would you go? What would you do? Take the first step toward making it happen.

the resolutionary war

Do you fight the Resolutionary War every January? Do you struggle with setting goals and keeping them for the year? Are you like me? I resolve, as the New Year begins, to lose weight, to start exercising, and to be nicer. I resolve that *this* year—for sure—will *finally* be the year I get it all together.

And it works! Until January third. By the end of that first week of January, I've failed miserably. I've slid back into the same old patterns. The ideal is elusive, proving impossible once again. I drown my feelings of self-loathing in the left-over Christmas fudge. I'm sick of it, aren't you? (The frustration, not the fudge.)

Next January first will be different. Next year I won't feel like a failure for not losing weight, not exercising, and not becoming a nicer human being. Next January you won't find me wallowing in the swamp of self-recrimination. No sirree! Next January first will be different, because this year I've made a list of resolutions I can live with. Here it is:

Resolution 1: This Year I Will Let Myself Go

I'm letting myself go this year. I'm facing facts. I'll never have a chiseled torso, sculpted calves, or abs of steel. I'll never run a marathon—unless the twenty-six miles a day I used to cover chasing after toddlers counts.

I'm letting myself go. Who cares if my buns of marshmallow sag at the beach? I'll never see those people again anyway. Who cares if my thighs jiggle when I tap dance? The Rockettes all have the same problem, eventually. I hope.

I'm letting myself go. I'm going to stop being so self-conscious, so afraid of what others will think. This year I'm going to risk something, try something new. I might tackle that challenging Chopin piano prelude, read *War and Peace*, or learn to dance the two-step. I might just write a novel, write bad poetry, or take up basket weaving, no matter what someone else might think. Who knows what I might discover if I just let myself go.

I might find myself on stage at the comedy club on open-mike night. Will the world come to an end if I tell a joke that bombs? I might find myself in front of an easel, painting awful pictures. Will the planets stop their course if I lack talent? I might take a chance and try in-line skating. So what if I'm a klutz? So what if the emergency-room doctor thinks I'm an idiot? I'll—hopefully—never see that doctor again.

Letting *myself* go, I might start thinking more about *others*. I might volunteer to help somebody or give more time—maybe even more money—to good causes. I might become more grateful and catch myself raising my voice—maybe even my hands—in church in praise of God.

This year I'm letting myself go, no matter what others think. I'm setting myself free.

Resolution 2: This Year I Will Sleep More

I've missed a lot of sleep tossing and turning, thinking about everything I should be doing instead of sleeping. This year I'm changing that.

This year I'm establishing a bedtime routine that begins at noon with a ban on caffeine. I'm going to start unwinding early in the evening with calming activities like reading and soft music. At bedtime I'll ease into the sack, and instead of tossing and turning, fretting over all I've failed to do, I'll congratulate myself on all I've managed to accomplish. Even if all I did was keep breathing. I'll forgive myself for whatever I've left undone. I'll take some deep, relaxing breaths, and as I do, I'll thank God for the gift of the day and his many blessings, and I'll leave tomorrow to itself.

On those nights when I do happen to be awake in the wee hours, worrying about my children and their future, about wars and rumors of wars, I'm going to remember that those things are out of my control. I'm resolving to pray more in the middle of the night, giving those worries to God, the only one who can do something about it all.

Resolution 3: This Year I Will Slow Down

Why am I in such a hurry? Where am I rushing? What am I missing as I rush on by? My grandchildren aren't going to be little children for very long. I already rushed through the childhood of my own children. Why were we in such a hurry?

I pushed my children into after-school activities, cramming their schedules so full of commitments they hardly had time to breathe. One late summer day, as we discussed our options for the coming school year, my fourth-grade daughter asked, "Mom, why can't we just come home after school and play with our friends?"

Why indeed? We cut the commitments way down. I worried a little that my children would turn into worthless, idle bums, but missing out on all those organized activities didn't hurt them one bit; in fact, it seems that it freed them to find their own interests. One is an extreme sports enthusiast, into mountain-bike racing, snowboarding, and rock climbing. Another is a tennis player with a head for business. Another is an artist and a writer. They found their own way. And the best part is, by the time they did, they were old enough to drive themselves there.

What will happen if I slow down? Will I find time after work to just play with my friends? What will I discover if I slow down? I might sense the passage of time more acutely, become more keenly aware of how fleeting my days are. I might be inspired to take special care not to waste another moment in meaningless busyness.

I might spend more time talking with my mother, while I still can. I might take more walks up the road to stand at the top of our hill and look out over the valley below, breathing there in what we call "the God Spot," enjoying the magnificent creation God has set before us, around us, and in us.

I might spend more time staring out my window at the wintry garden, imagining the tulips, now dormant under the frozen ground, waiting, as I am, for spring. I might hope.

Who says every moment has to be "productive"?

Resolution 4: This Year I Will Take More Time Off

I thought taking more time off would be easy when I left my corporate job to work from home. But my new boss—that's me—works me harder than any corporate slave driver could. At home it's too easy to slip back into the office after dinner, or on weekends, or in the middle of the night when I can't sleep. It's all too easy to work straight through lunch when there are no coworkers inviting me out for a burger.

But how creative am I after ten hours at my desk? How sensitive am I to my children or my spouse after a fourteen-hour day? How much creativity or sensitivity can I wring from a dried-up sponge?

What I need is more time off—every day—to soak up new joy and fresh energy. Time to play the piano, read something just for fun, laugh with the family, take a walk, or just relax with my favorite music and a cup of something warm and wonderful.

This year I resolve to work my set hours and then stop. At the end of work, I'm going to close the office door and walk out into my life. Work—the project, the book writing, or the laundry—can wait.

I'm resolving to enjoy my time off with family and friends. I'll savor my evenings and my weekends. I'm going to celebrate the Sabbath. Working six days a week is enough! I'm going to respect the boundaries between work and play. And this year I'm taking a *real* vacation. I've earned it, and I *won't* spend it working on the house.

Resolution 5: This Year I Will Eat Dessert First

"Don't fill up on those cookies, or you won't have room for dinner," our mothers used to tell us. What kind of a threat was that? What normal kid would respond, "Gosh, Mom, I didn't realize what I was doing! Of course I want to have room for the brussels sprouts. I'll stop eating this chocolate-chip cookie right now." Fat chance. A normal kid will take the cookie every time. And I'm a normal kid.

All my life I've heard that nagging little voice in my head (can you hear it too?) that tells me I have to clean my plate before I can have dessert. ("We would have loved to have so much to eat during the Depression!") I have to finish my brussels sprouts before I get to the good stuff. ("All those starving children . . .") Well, I'm through listening to that little nag, as of this year.

What if I never get to dessert? What if my life is demanded of me this day? I don't know which meal will be my last. I imagine a woman like me saying as the *Titanic* was sinking, "If I'd known this was going to happen, I'd have eaten my dessert at dinner last night!" That's so sad. I'm eating my dessert first from now on.

Dessert is the reward of life, the delicious, satisfying, sweet treat in life. I'm not waiting until the end to have it. I'm not saving it until I've been through all the icky stuff. While I'm at it, I'm done saving the good dishes, the good napkins, and my good underwear. I'm going to start using those things now, and while I do, I'll be thanking God and celebrating his blessings in my life.

I'm calling a truce this year in the Resolutionary War. Next January first I'll be smiling, because things are going to be different from now on. This year I'm letting myself go. I'm going to be satisfied with who I am. This year I'll be sleeping more, rocking in the cradle of God's tender care. This year I'll be slowing down. I'm giving myself permission to do *half* as much and to take *twice* as long doing it. This year I'll be taking more time off. I'm giving myself permission to do less than I am humanly capable of doing. And this year, I'll be eating my dessert first.

This year, at last, I have a list I can live—*truly live*—with!

> May he give you the desire of your heart
> and make all your plans succeed.
> —Psalm 20:4

points to ponder

1. How good are you at keeping resolutions? What resolutions have you made in the past? What have you learned about yourself?

2. If you could make and keep one, and only one, resolution for the rest of your life, what would it be and why would you make it?

3. What is your biggest regret in life? Write it on a piece of paper. Tell God about it and then rip, shred, or burn (safely—you don't want to have to regret burning the house down) the paper. As you destroy the paper, release that regret to God. What's done is done. You are free! Celebrate!

true

part two

confessions

waking up

The best part of waking up is Folgers in your cup . . ."

My favorite commercial. I love coffee. Hot, smooth caffeine in fun mugs. "She who laughs lasts," says one of my favorite mugs. Another favorite is painted with dancing monkeys. A great cup is part of the whole coffee experience.

I have four delicate china cups with matching saucers that I received from an employer when I lived in New York. They'd come from a grand old hotel, and legend has it that General Douglas MacArthur may have once drunk coffee from these very cups. As I sip from one of these cups, it's 1943 and I'm in a USO canteen in New York. My hair's in a chignon, my shoulder pads are huge, and the seams in my precious nylon stockings are straight. I'm listening to big-band music, waiting for someone to ask me to fox-trot. I'm my mother.

I buy souvenir coffee mugs in airports when I travel. Back home, I sit and sip and reminisce. One mug takes me back to Los Angeles, another to Atlanta. Matching mugs bring back memories of Disney World as Terry and I sit and sip, he from his Mickey Mouse "Big Cheese" mug and I from my Minnie mug, his "Main Squeeze." Perhaps someday mugs will carry me back to even more exotic places—Rome, Paris, Fargo.

I love my cups, but it's what's inside them that really gets my heart a-fluttering. Literally. I love coffee. I love the smell of the beans in the coffee aisle at the grocery store. Isn't Juan Valdez cute? I started buying and grinding my own beans years ago, just to sniff the aroma as they're pulverized.

One of my favorite rewards for working hard is a trip to the local bookstore-cum-coffeehouse for my special order, a combination café mocha and latté, with extra chocolate and double whipped cream. I love the aromatic potions with the exotic names at the espresso bar. Papuan Peaberry. Madagascar Mud. Ethiopian Eye Opener. Kenyan Kazowie.

On a trip to Ecuador, I loved the thick, dark brew cut with milk—*café con leche*—served each morning. I loved the young Ecuadorian waiter practicing his English on my husband with a labored, "Coffee, meester? With meelk?" The waiter grinned with pride. He'd mastered the most important foreign phrase in my book.

Plain or fancy, I love coffee in any incarnation. I love it black. I love it with cream and sugar. I loved the pale coffee, so pale you could see the bottom of the cup through it, that my aunt Mabel used to make. How elegantly she poured coffee from her china cup into her saucer, melted a sugar cube in it, and sipped.

Any grade, any shade—I love coffee.

I've loved the smell since childhood, when in the morning the *pop-popping* of the percolator on the kitchen counter mixed with the sounds of my parents' discussion of the morning paper's crossword puzzle. My father's aftershave mingled with the rich aroma from the coffeepot. Coffee smells like home to me. I'll buy a bushel of beans if I ever find a blend of Kona with a hint of Old Spice.

When we studied South America in sixth-grade social studies, we drew outline maps of the countries on that continent. I got to glue the coffee beans to Colombia. That's the most important thing I learned that year. Coffee came from Colombia. Those lucky, lucky Colombians.

I couldn't wait until I was old enough to drink coffee. I recall vividly the time in my freshman year of college when I made myself a percolatorful, poured myself that first adult cup, and sat down to study. I had arrived at last, and I've been hooked ever since.

I don't just love coffee; I *need* coffee. I crave it, yearn for it, and seek it out. I confess my addiction, but I won't be shaking the habit anytime soon. I'm just not myself without my brew. I don't function in the morning until the caffeine kicks in. Before coffee, I'm a zombie wandering the house, stumbling to the kitchen to fill a mug. I then sit and sip the first glorious mouthful. *Ahh . . . The best part of waking up . . .* The cobwebs start to clear. The fog lifts. This is coffee. This is living.

What does it take to wake you up?

I experienced another kind of waking up the day I stole Bobby Hon's dog. I was five years old, walking down the sidewalk in our city neighborhood. On the front step of Bobby's house down the block sat his stuffed toy dog. This was no ordinary stuffed pup. This was a big, fuzzy, flop-eared mutt at least half my size.

Bobby had left it on his steps. I took it and ran home.

A dog that size was not an easy thing to conceal, so I hid it outside, tucked behind a planter at the front entryway of our apartment building. I went inside. I didn't dare bring the

dog into the apartment, for stealing it had awakened something in me, a fierce monster growling, *This isn't right. This is
wrong! Wrong!*

Pinocchio was lucky to have the patient Jiminy Cricket to
help him. This was no gentle friend inside of me, no chirping,
cheery chum offering singsong reminders to be good. This
monster of mine growled the whole time I sat eating my supper and tormented me as I sat watching television. *Stealer! Bad!*

I wish there was such a thing as kindergarten altruism. I
wish I could say that at the tender age of five, what awakened in me was a sense of compassion. That the thought of
poor Bobby sobbing to his mother in grief compelled me to
return that dog. That would have been noble. But that wasn't
the case.

I felt none of that kind of regret. I saw one toy dog and
two kids. He had the dog and I did not, and of the two of us,
I thought it was better if he was the one crying.

No, it wasn't nobility or compassion that caused my
awakening. It was the fiery ignition of conscience—the monster unleashed in me—and with it, raw fear and the specter
of parental disapproval. My parents—bless them!—had obviously taught me right from wrong. Stealing was wrong, and
I knew it. (I dimly recall a prior incident involving candy at
the corner grocery, my sticky fingers, and my mother's angry
voice.) I had left the dog outside on our front stoop because I
had stolen it and I didn't want to be caught—*Stop, thief!*—by
my parents.

I've wondered how this happens. How does the toddler
learn the difference between sharing and stealing? Where and
when is the line formed? How is it drawn? What sparks the
conscience? I've wondered about those among us "without
conscience"—the serial killers, the habitual thieves. Is their

conscience nonexistent, or was its seed warped by environment? Such questions are the lifework of many criminologists: Is the criminal mind born or made?

Here's what I know about it: I stole Bobby Hon's dog and felt bad about it. I had coveted my neighbor's dog. I was guilty. I'd taken the apple and eaten it. Someone was watching. I was naked and I was afraid. Very afraid.

I didn't need to be taught to steal, to envy, to lie, or to cheat. I came by it naturally. We all do. "Surely I was sinful at birth, sinful from the time my mother conceived me" is the biblical lament in Psalm 51:5. I certainly was sinful. The puppy behind the planter was proof.

The effect of my conscience waking up was swift and sure. After an hour or so of restless, guilty pondering and trying to silence the monster, I ran back outside, grabbed the purloined pup, and raced it back to Bobby's house. I hurled the stuffed dog onto his steps like it was a live grenade and ran for home.

And the monster smiled.

The system worked. (Thanks, Mom and Dad.) Parents have a duty to society to create decent citizens, to teach right from wrong, to shape discernment, and to instill healthy respect for authority. And God is there from day one, isn't he, whispering to the folks, helping in the parenting? Yes. God wakes us up.

"Surely you desire truth in the inner parts; you teach me wisdom in the inmost place" (Psalm 51:6). Conscience. Not a monster at all, but rather God's wisdom and truth in our inmost place.

God woke me up. *Don't keep the dog. It's wrong.*

We wake up in stages, it seems. It begins with sharing the grocer's candy without his permission and learning the difference between borrowing and stealing. Then a stuffed dog brings irresistible temptation, a choice to steal outright, and a test of the will. A battle of lust versus virtue, good versus evil—Armageddon in microcosm, waged again and again.

Other awakenings, other battles follow. To cheat or not to cheat in school, at Monopoly, at baseball, on your tax return, on your spouse. To take or not to take staples from the office, bath towels from the hotel, or pay for days you weren't really sick. To tell the truth and weather the financial storm or to overstate corporate earnings and defraud investors. To seek the common good or just the bottom line. To keep or return a found wallet. To keep or give back extra change received at the grocery store.

Have you noticed that our natural inclination is to go our own way? "There is a path before each person that seems right, but it ends in death" (Proverbs 16:25 NLT). If we are wise, we listen to wisdom, we learn to respect authority, and we learn where the line between right and wrong is drawn.

Where do you draw the line?

I went to the local Target just after Christmas. I picked up six large plastic storage bins for some postholiday organizing. (Yes, another new plan!) The clerk rang up five of the bins.

"You missed one," I told her. She zapped the bar code again. It seemed that she missed again, but by then, I was paying the total and leaving the store.

Halfway to the door, I heard the familiar voice. *You didn't pay for that sixth bin.* Out in the parking lot, packing my purchases into the trunk, I heard it again, louder, firmer. *You didn't pay what you owe.*

"But," I argued, "I tried. I gave her the chance to charge me. She blew it. I'm not guilty. It's not my fault!" The voice was gentle then. *You know better.*

The voice was right. I did know better. I headed back into the store to Customer Service and insisted they take another four dollars and ninety-nine cents plus tax. The system works.

What a gift God has given us—this voice that directs us, this Spirit that desires what is right and good. This ever-present Guide and Counselor, ready to steer us toward the path of right. Ready to help us turn from our own way—the way leading to destruction—toward the way that leads to life. Ready to speak truth and wisdom if we are ready to listen. Ready to forgive us by grace as we repent.

What a gift this voice, this Spirit, this presence—this God conscience—like a good, strong cup of coffee. We drink deep and the cobwebs clear. The fog lifts. We wake up.

> Search me, O God, and know my heart;
>   test me and know my anxious thoughts.
> See if there is any offensive way in me,
>   and lead me in the way everlasting.
>   —Psalm 139:23–24

points to ponder

1. Describe a time when you felt your conscience at work. How did you respond?

2. Is there an ultimate standard for right and wrong, or is such judgment relative, as some claim? What do you think? Is it ever okay to steal or to lie? Is it ever okay for someone to steal from you or to lie to you?

3. Describe a moral dilemma you've faced (for example, feeling torn between telling the truth and protecting someone). How did you handle the situation? What did you learn from it?

the highway book nook

Floyd B. Olson Memorial Highway ran through our north Minneapolis neighborhood. This four-lane highway was the route that took us—by bus, car, bicycle, or walking—downtown to the east, and west to the city lakes. Long before the mini-malls, suburban shopping centers, and superstores appeared, small mom-and-pop grocery stores, drugstores, hardware stores, meat markets, and bakeries lined the south side of the divided highway. All within walking distance of home. Anyplace we needed to go, we could go via Olson Highway. It was the thoroughfare of our lives.

The highway was divided by a wide, grassy median, long since removed to accommodate the heavy traffic flowing from the suburbs into the city these days. On one block of that median was a statue of Floyd B. Olson—the Honorable!—former governor of Minnesota. My friend Cary and I packed peanut butter and jelly sandwiches and a thermos of red Kool-Aid and rode our bikes to the statue for picnics. It was summer. We were nine years old.

After lunch we'd cross the eastbound half of the highway to a tiny store jammed between other tiny stores, a store called the Highway Book Nook. The Book Nook had that dusty smell that accumulates after decades of cramming too much stuff into too little space. The cramped storefront with the warped wooden floorboards was packed with merchandise. Blouses and socks, dishes and doilies, greeting cards and oilcloth. (Oilcloth? How old am I?)

And there were toys. At the front window stood a long, low counter with small, open wooden boxes on top. Each box held a different kind of toy. Tops and jacks, toy soldiers and balls, yo-yos and metal cars, modeling clay and Chinese finger traps, whistles and hand buzzers. Some of that stuff shows up these days on the *Antiques Roadshow* and is worth a small fortune. If only we'd known.

We looked, we touched, but we rarely bought. Ours was a poor neighborhood. We were poor children. Below the toy counter was, for me, the Holy Grail of toydom. There, set in a vertical display, were the paper dolls. I knelt often before the paper dolls, worshiping. I dreamed of owning them all. I made my rare purchases carefully, with the shrewdness of Rockefeller buying another oil field.

Would it be sweet, dimpled little Shirley Temple? (Her ruffled dresses were so beautiful.) Wholesome and sturdy teenage Judy Garland or deadeye Annie Oakley? Or would it be the glamorous June Allyson, who came with two different swimsuits? (Isn't June advertising adult diapers or something these days? Hmm.) These were huge decisions. Agonizing choices.

I imagine they also sold books at the Highway Book Nook. I don't recall seeing any, but I was only a kid. The store was owned by two old women (in their fifties probably; ha!), who

I assume were sisters. The Book Nook was just a front, a way to support their real work. They were missionaries, and we, the children of the inner city, the great unwashed, uncombed mass of juvenile sinners—we were their mission field.

It was in the back room of the Highway Book Nook, which was separated from the storefront by a faded curtain, where I first heard about Jesus. Once a week after school, the sisters pulled the curtain aside and admitted us, wild beasts of the streets, to their sanctuary.

Sitting on one of several wooden benches—salvaged church pews perhaps—I first heard the songs of the faith. There in the back room, behind the business end of the store, the sisters conducted their real business. For the Book Nook sisters believed with all their hearts—I see it now—that they'd been sent to this city, to this neighborhood, to this street, to this humble, stuffy little building, to save our souls.

That summer when I was nine, the sisters offered vacation Bible school to the neighborhood. For five mornings in July, I rode my bike to the Book Nook and there experienced "Sunday school" for the first time. Our family didn't go to church. Sitting in the back room that July, in the oppressive heat, I colored, cut, and pasted pictures from Bible stories. I'd never heard the stories connected with the pictures before, and I loved every minute of this time. I loved school, and this was school in the summer.

We were to learn a Bible verse that week, as any good church school curriculum requires. The verse I memorized was this one, from the King James Bible: "For God so loved the world, that he gave his only begotten Son, that whosoever believeth in him should not perish, but have everlasting life" (John 3:16 KJV). Quite a mouthful for a nine-year-old. For anyone.

I had never heard these words before. We didn't talk about God or the Bible at our house. I didn't know there was anything other than crude earth and tangible, touchable things. I didn't know there was a spiritual world until the Book Nook sisters showed it to me. Not until they invited me into the back of the store.

A few weeks later, in August, the sisters invited four of us girls, all alumni of the Highway Book Nook vacation Bible school program, to spend a weekend at a cabin on Prior Lake, south of Minneapolis (then a wilderness, now a suburb). I suppose this is what the sisters believed they should do with poor inner-city children in the summer—take us away from the traffic on the highway, away from the noise and distraction of city living. Take us into the country, into the fresh air. And our parents agreed.

The shoreline of the lake was green with algae and thick with lily pads. Dog days. With the high whine of katydids in the air and mosquitoes hovering like a cloud around us, we waded into the water, green slime clinging to our skin. We held our breath and swam out past the slime, coming up when we were clear of the weeds.

Our mothers had warned us not to swim during dog days. Neighborhood legend blamed dog-day swimming for everything from impetigo to polio. But we swam, the four of us, in water warm as a bath, which offered little relief from the relentless, buzzing heat. Horseflies nipped at any parts of our flesh not underwater. We splashed at them, squealing and diving, swimming the sticky afternoon away.

That night the four of us paired off in two double beds. I lay next to my friend Diana, whose family attended a church in our neighborhood. I'd seen her on Sunday mornings, dressed up. Diana knew all about Jesus. As we lay in the dark giggling, one of the Book Nook sisters came and stood in the doorway. I can see her still, silhouetted against the bare light-bulb out in the cabin's kitchen. She glowed.

She asked into the darkness, "Is there anyone here who has never invited Jesus into her heart?"

Had I ever done that? Not to my recollection. I was only nine. I hadn't yet done enough in life to have forgotten doing something that seemed so important.

I said, "I haven't."

The sister asked through the dark, "Would you like to?" *Would I?* The universe held its breath. I heard nothing but my own heart pounding.

"Yes," I whispered back. The Book Nook sister invited me to pray with her then, repeating what she said. I don't remember the exact words I prayed. Admitted I was a sinner. *Was I really?* Yes. Bobby's dog told me so. Admitted I needed Jesus. *Who didn't need God?* Asked him to forgive me, invited him into my heart. *A room was there, just for him.*

There are spectacular—miraculous—moments in life when the divine crashes into the mundane. The Bible is full of such moments. Noah hearing the command of God. Moses and the burning bush. Jacob wrestling in the middle of the night. Elijah on the mountain, receiving angelic ministrations, hearing the still, small voice. The seas parting, Lazarus coming forth from the tomb, blind men seeing. God at work in our world. Spectacular.

There are spectacular moments in life, I'm convinced, when the Spirit of God visits us personally, changing us forever. At such a time, our need is so great, our cry so honest, that God ordains the moment, clears a path through our resistance and doubt, through our ignorance and fear, and enters into our reality.

Lying in that cabin at Prior Lake on that hot August night, with my whispered "Amen," I sensed an invasion into my spirit. The entrance of someone distinct from me and unmistakably foreign to me—foreign until that moment when I felt the merging of our hearts. A binding, a renewal . . .

Oh, what is the word, Lord? What is the word to describe that moment of sudden clarity, of bright awareness that all of what I'd heard was true? That moment when I was suddenly certain that there was a God and that he loved me. That he had indeed sent his "only begotten Son" and that I had become one "whosoever believeth."

Knowing. That's the word. Knowing.

Suddenly knowing that a place existed where no highway could take me, that there was a journey—begun with a choice, a decision—only the heart could make. Suddenly knowing that another world existed, beyond Chinese finger traps and paper dolls, beyond school and the neighborhood.

Do you know the place? Have you made the journey yourself?

Suddenly knowing this all-encompassing, complete love. This sweetest, deepest tenderness. Was I aware at that moment how amazingly sweet, how unfathomably deep, God's love is? Only to the extent a child can understand such things. Years passed before I could begin to appreciate what God did for me on that stuffy August night. The night he parted the curtain and showed me the truth. The night he saved me.

Has the curtain parted for you? Are you among the "whosoever"? Have you experienced the sweet tenderness of God? Do you know how much he loves you? Do you know how much he longs to draw you close? He's waiting, right now, to tell you.

Listen for a moment.

I have loved you with an everlasting love;
I have drawn you with loving-kindness.
—Jeremiah 31:3

points to ponder

1. Describe your favorite childhood place. What made it so special?

2. Who made the biggest impression on you as a child? How are you different as a result of having known that person? (Write a thank-you note to someone who had a positive influence on you.)

3. Who taught you about God when you were a child? What did you learn? What do you think about God today? How would you describe your relationship with him?

thunder

June Cleaver, in her pearls and crisply ironed dress, her hair perfectly coifed (like every great television mother of the 1960s), greets her hubby, Ward, at the door when he comes home in the evening. Ward has had a hard day at the office but still looks morning fresh in his suit and tie. A great television dad. Looks good. Comes straight home from work.

Ward gives June a peck on the cheek. She asks him how his day went. He asks her about their two sons, and she says, "Ward, I think you're going to have to have a talk with the Beaver."

Oh, that pesky little guy. What's that rascal done this time? What family crisis will they have to resolve in this episode? Are his parents upset because they think Beaver spent all his savings on something for himself? (It turns out he was buying something for someone less fortunate. What a relief.) Is it that his friends have led him astray? (Beaver learns in a half hour to resist peer pressure. Thank goodness.) Is it that the Beav has been fighting with a classmate? (It turns out to be a misunderstanding with a nice little girl who's just moved to the neighborhood. Whew!)

Whatever the crisis, there are sure to be smiles all around at the end of thirty minutes. That's how things work for the Cleavers. And at Ozzie and Harriet's house. And in the Brady home. What adjectives describe these households? Perfect? Almost. Idyllic? Yes. Surreal? Yes, completely surreal.

I didn't live with the Cleavers. At 7:30 p.m. on a Thursday night when I was ten, I hid in my bedroom in our apartment. Two French doors—my bedroom doors—sheltered me from the fight going on in the living room. The doors had two missing panes of glass on the bottom row of the left-hand door. My older brother had accidentally lobbed a bowling ball through the glass as he demonstrated his five-step approach one day; the two panes of glass and the wood frame between them had been demolished by his deadly aim. I heard everything as my parents argued.

They fought that night about his drinking. About their money problems. He shouted and swore. She threw a hand mirror at him. It sailed across the room and smashed into a thousand shards. I heard it. Cold. Shattering. I saw the remains later.

My father's voice thundered, angry. My mother's response was shrill, arguing back, and then her voice dropped lower, threatening. I slumped against the wall next to the French doors and held my hands to my ears. Thunder crashed around me.

I wanted to thunder back, "Stop! Don't say these things. Don't upset each other. Just pretend!" Instead I picked up a book and began to read. I picked up a pen and began to write. I wrote and wrote about different lives and better places, where there was less thunder and more smiling. Much more

smiling. I read and I wrote for years and years. I'm still reading and writing.

My childhood was unpredictable. My father loved music
and poetry; he read everything and had a great sense of
humor. He played the piano and sang. He was a gifted crafts-
man, carpenter, and electrician. He loved us—my mother, my
brothers, my sister, and me. My father was also an alcoholic,
a broken, sad man whose life didn't turn out the way he had
dreamed it would.

Life was unpredictable. One night Dad is sitting at the
dining-room table playing Yahtzee with us, laughing and
smiling. The next night he's sitting at the same dining-room
table drunk and spouting philosophy, warning us about the
traps of life. One day we are all together on a family vacation,
fishing on a lake, whole and happy. The next day Dad is
drinking and there are no more vacations, no money for anything, and I am learning what lies to tell the bill collectors on
the phone. I'm learning how to pretend there is no thunder,
only blue and sunny skies.

One night we are at the public library, and my father studies books on electricity and plumbing, learning, teaching himself to be better. I am wandering the stacks in the children's
room, congratulating myself on having read everything in the
Picture Books and Junior Readers sections, looking for the
next adventure.

The next night Dad is in a bar, and I am shivering out in
the car in the dark, waiting for him to come out. Later I have
a nightmare that I have to drive the car home but I cannot
reach the pedals or see above the steering wheel. In my dream
my little brother is in the back seat. His life is in my hands. I
am responsible.

One night we are at Aunt Mabel's, and she and Dad are drinking coffee. She sets that lump of sugar on her saucer, pours coffee into it, lets it cool, and then sips. They laugh and talk. Dad is "on the wagon." My brothers and I are in the living room, on the fat sofa, listening to a story on the record player, following along in a picture book of *The Tortoise and the Hare*. *Ding!* Time to turn the page. The hare sleeps while the tortoise heads down the trail. *Ding!* Turn the page and learn that slow and steady wins the race.

Ding! Turn the page and Dad is off the wagon. He's asleep outside in the car, where he has been sleeping all night long, too drunk last night to make it upstairs to the apartment. All the neighbors see him there. *Ding!* Turn the page, please.

Please.

Day and night. Sunshine and rain. Fair and foul. Calm and storm. And thunder . . . thunder . . . thunder.

What adjectives describe your childhood? If you had a childhood anything like mine, you might have trouble finding the right words to describe it. You might have been told that you were not allowed to tell the truth about your life, about what happened. You might have been told that you had to cover things up. That you had to keep secrets.

It's time to tell the truth if you haven't told it before. It's time to let God set your spirit free from your past.

What is your life like today? Are you still keeping secrets, still hiding your pain? Are you living your nightmares today?

It's time to tell the truth. It's time to let God set you free from the past. It's time to have a future.

Our past often affects our view of God. How does God look to you today? Author Max Lucado says we each have a window in our heart. The window starts out clear, until a pebble—a pain in life—hits the window and cracks the glass. We now see God through that broken window.

What pebbles have cracked your glass? What rocks have fractured your view of God? Enough cracks—poverty, disease, divorce, frustration, addiction—and God looks like Picasso painted him. Lines askew and a twisted expression. Cruel. Mocking.

Who would trust a God who looked like that? For a time, looking through the glass cracked by poverty, alcoholism, divorce, and other pain, God appeared to me to be unreliable and unpredictable. If not downright unable, he was certainly unwilling to provide what I needed. He appeared to be fickle, ready to dump me for someone he thought was more lovable. He seemed to have a standard he hadn't revealed to me, a standard for who was acceptable and who was not. A secret standard that defined "worthy." A standard I fell short of.

But God has given me a new piece of glass—one that is pebble-proof. The glass surrounds me, an "invisible protective shield," like the toothpaste commercials used to promise. I'm learning what it means that God loves me with an everlasting, never-changing love. He's dependable and consistent. He is not fickle but is the most dedicated and true lover imaginable. He loved me before I drew my first breath. He loved me completely and absolutely before I had ever done one thing in this life. He loved me from the start and will continue to love me, no matter what.

God loves me in poverty and in wealth, in sickness and in health, in focused times and when I am adrift. Whatever happens, wherever I am, however I am behaving, God loves me. And he loves you the same way. We have trouble understanding God's love because we have no earthly models.

Nobody comes close to loving us as God does. Human beings simply can't love like God loves.

Let me say that again. People cannot love us with the unconditional love we need. Only God can.

I'm learning to be at peace with the past. God drew me out of the storm, drew me with tender kindness into the arms of faith. He drew me out from under the clouds of darkness, depression, and discouragement into a bright and spacious place. He led me out of the pain and struggle into the sweet sunshine of his love and care. God is setting me free from my past. Free to live in the present. Free to believe in a future.

But I wonder, what about you, dear reader, who may be in the middle of the storm? What about you, whose glass has been shattered by heartache, whose view is obscured by tears? What about you who are feeling rejected, worthless, hopeless, helpless? You, deafened by the thunder, pounded by the pain, drowning in the deluge of grief?

You need to know, sweet friend, that God loves you. He cares about you as you listen to the thunder.

Oh, please hear this: God cares about you. He is there with you in the middle of your heartache, your pain, your grief. Talk to him. Tell him what's on your mind. Pour out your heart.

God cares about you. You've carried your burden long enough. It's time to lay it down.

Just lay it down.

> When the kindness and love of God our Savior appeared,
> he saved us, not because of righteous things we had done,
> but because of his mercy.
>
> —Titus 3:4–5

points to ponder

1. When you were growing up, was your family perfect like the Cleavers? Blended like the Brady Bunch? Or just plain freaky like the Addams Family? How so?

2. Quickly, without giving it too much thought, list ten words that describe your childhood. Did you discover any surprises? (If you like to write, try freewriting for five or more minutes starting with, "My childhood was . . .")

3. What pebbles have cracked your glass? What do you think today about what you've experienced? What does God have to say about it? Talk to a trusted professional if you need to. You've carried the pain long enough. It's time to let God set you free from the past.

box lunch

I didn't know about the church-picnic dress code before that Sunday in August when Diana invited me to her church's picnic. I'd dressed for this picnic as I would for any other—in shorts and a T-shirt.

The church women were resplendent, having just come from Sunday services. Diana's always beautiful mother, Zona, was particularly beautiful that day, her deep yellow dress and matching wide-brimmed hat setting off her light chocolate skin. Diana herself was a sight to behold in a ruffled pink dress and nylons—nylons at age nine!—that made her brown legs look pink. She'd never looked fancier. I'd never felt plainer.

Diana had told me to bring a box lunch. "Be sure to decorate it," she said. "They're giving prizes for the best decorating." I had no idea what a box lunch was. I found an old shoebox. I made myself a peanut butter sandwich. I don't remember what else I put in the box. An apple maybe. Then I scrounged around the house for something to decorate the box with. I figured I would decorate the box with things about God. This was a church picnic, after all, the first church picnic I'd ever been invited to attend. I wanted to make a good impression.

The only magazines I could find were some copies of *Reader's Digest* and a few *Mechanics Illustrated*, neither of which were known for great photography. What I wouldn't have given for a copy of *National Geographic* that day. I found a couple of pictures of flowers in the *Digest* and a bird or two. Since I'd recently learned that God had made everything, these pictures fit my theme. I cut them out and stuck them to the sides and top of the box with homemade paste of flour and water. (I always made my own paste. To keep the paste from getting rancid, my mother added a few drops from a tiny bottle of oil of wintergreen. I love wintergreen LifeSavers today because they smell like that paste.)

The pictures stuck in place, I labored to print on the side of the box the only other thing I knew about Jesus. It was the Bible verse I'd memorized at the Book Nook, the only verse I'd discovered to date—John 3:16. The verse that talked about how much God loved me and how he'd sent Jesus to save me. It was my most important verse. Still is.

Oh, the feast at that picnic! When lunch is served in heaven, it will be like that picnic. Tablecloths spread across the long concrete tables in the park were covered with bowls of potato salad and corn on the cob, pans of home-fried chicken, frosted cakes, and plates of cookies. And dozens of picnic baskets, beautifully woven and bedecked with ribbons and bows. And plunked among them, my shoebox.

I remember that box lunch every once in a while, usually when I'm sitting in church admiring someone's new outfit or pretty dress. I remember it when I've spent a little too much time fussing with my own appearance on a Sunday morning.

When I've been tempted to buy a new outfit not because I need it but just to have it. When I'm caught up in appearances, in how we all look on the outside, I'll think about that box lunch and I'll blush, knowing what I know now.

I was a waif, a pauper. Too poor to buy real paste. Too poor for a fancy basket with ribbons and bows. Too poor for a ruffled dress and nylons. I imagine how adults at some other picnic might have clucked their tongues in pity and whispered behind my back, "Look at that sorry little thing." I myself have looked at others that way at times.

I remember that box lunch and I blush, because I felt *none* of that at that picnic. If they snickered, I didn't hear it. If they judged me, I didn't sense it. I felt no snide condemnation, no clucking pity, no sorrowful shame on that August afternoon in Glenwood Park with God's good people.

Maybe they knew what it was like to be judged on appearance. Maybe they looked at me as Jesus did. Jesus said, "Let the little children come to me, and do not hinder them, for the kingdom of heaven belongs to such as these" (Matthew 19:14). It was as if they'd heard Jesus saying that and listened, as if he himself were right there in their midst.

I felt their wide grace that bright Sunday, and in it, God's shining love—the expanse of it. Enormous. Unfathomable. I sensed his complete acceptance of me, just the way I was, in that group of his people, in their warm smiles, in the food they shared. Especially the angel food cake. Jesus told them, "I was hungry and you gave me something to eat" (Matthew 25:35). They'd listened to that too.

I was hungry that day. His people fed me. I was a pauper in the royal court, a waif with her hand out, begging bread, begging love. Jesus was there, wrapping me in brown arms and making me feel like part of the family.

When have I done that? Who do I know who needs that today? The woman on the street, pushing the grocery cart full of newspapers. The man with the burlap sack, trudging the ditches in search of aluminum cans. The man with AIDS, marked and scarred and dying. The little girl with vacant eyes, bruised and sad, in the back row. The old woman slumped in the chair at the nursing home, mumbling someone's name. The young mom in the grocery store, shaking her child in frustration, badly in need of a break. The toothless grandmother in Ecuador at the intersection, coming to the car window with cup in hand, begging for pennies. The man next door whose son is in jail. The widow down the block. The divorced mother around the corner.

Who needs the touch of God today? Whose spirit needs to be fed?

When the baskets were judged, my shoebox won Honorable Mention. I'd never heard the term before. It sounded good. Really good. Olympic Gold would not have shone more brightly in my eyes. I knew it wasn't the box itself that had won me such high acclaim; I could see how sad it looked compared to all those fine baskets. I could see that it couldn't be the pictures; they looked pretty sorry. One of them was torn half off, and another was missing completely.

That left only one thing that could have earned such praise. It had to be the Bible verse. John 3:16 was the winning ticket! It was my ticket through the gate, the same ticket those loving people and the Book Nook sisters held. The only ticket worth holding.

That day I learned that God smiles with the same favor on the million-dollar offering and the widow's mite, when they're given with the right motivation. I learned that God doesn't play favorites. He didn't look at me with pity, didn't see me as a sorry little thing who couldn't afford real paste or a fancy dress.

We are all paupers in the court of the King. We are all waifs, our hands out, begging bread. We are lost, worn out, and weary. We are lepers, diseased and contagious. Unclean. We are shrewd and wary of strangers. Wary of anything that seems too good to be true. No such thing as a free lunch. We are delinquent rebels, bent on our own destruction. We are malevolent miscreants, hate-filled bigots, and shameless liars. We are unrepentant dolts. We are fools. Ridiculous fools.

At least that's what I am. Worthy of pity. Worthy of rejection. Worthy of hell. But God doesn't leave me there. He looks beyond appearances. He sees the heart. He sees the earnest child, looking to please, longing for love. He sees the child, wounded, lost, and afraid. He sees, deep, deep, the repentant spirit, the longing for redemption. He sees the child, longing to be healed.

And he, loving first, loving best, reaches out to her, in a little back room, behind a worn curtain, through his people, through his Word, to draw her near to his heart. He reaches out to her in a stuffy cabin, crashing into her small, bleak world and filling it with light. He reaches out to her again over a piece of cake, among his people on a sunny afternoon, drawing her close and feeding her spirit.

Decades later he reaches out to her over a cup of coffee in the quiet of her kitchen. She remembers warmly his touch, his love, and his acceptance of her. She offers up, again, her sorrow for sin and her gratitude for grace. She offers up to him her life, her hands, her body, and her prayers. Her heart.

He, loving first, loving best, accepts it all, without reservation. And with arms of infinite love, he draws her closer.

I led them with cords of human kindness,
　　with ties of love;
I lifted the yoke from their neck
　　and bent down to feed them.

—Hosea 11:4

points to ponder

1. Recall your childhood picnic memories. Detail the who, what, where, and when of those experiences. What other fond childhood memories can you recall? If you have children, what memories will they carry into the future? What memories would you like to create with them today?

2. Does it ever seem like God plays favorites? Does it seem like he answers prayer for some and not for others? What experiences have led you to think as you do about this? Can you find support in the Bible for your position?

3. When have you experienced God's unconditional love? When have his people shown you kindness? Who do you know who needs a touch of kindness today? Take action.

confessions of a prayer wimp

I heard it again today. A radio host introduced his female guest as "a real prayer warrior." I cringed with guilt, imagining this saint who has worn out countless pairs of pantyhose at the knee, praying for lost causes and hopeless cases. This saint whose eloquent prayers alter the course of history, change the minds of presidents, and avert disasters. This saint whose diligent prayers inspire prodigals homeward. In her shadow, I feel puny and pathetic, for you see, I'm not a prayer warrior at all. I'm a prayer wimp.

Problems like the water heater exploding don't send a prayer warrior running from the house, in her ratty pink bathrobe and fuzzy purple slippers, screaming, "Help, Lord! Save us!" No, a warrior never loses her cool like that.

"Thank you, Lord, for this opportunity to wash the basement floor," she intones. Rolling her eyes heavenward as she mops, she adds, "Oh, and the ceiling too."

And I know that if car trouble strands a warrior in the middle of nowhere, with an ice-cream cake melting in her back seat, she doesn't pound her forehead on the steering wheel and shout to the cornfields, "Why *me*, Lord?" A warrior remains calm, though she knows eight giggling fourth-grade girls are waiting back at the house with the birthday girl's anxious father.

No, the warrior doesn't panic. She smiles, praying for the birthday celebration and for the Good Samaritan tow-truck driver who will happen along before her cake thaws. And he'll refuse to accept her check as he tips his hat, insisting, "It's my pleasure to be of service, ma'am."

The tow truck shows up for me too, but much later, as I'm trying to dam the flow of melting ice cream with one used tissue and an old receipt I've dislodged from the gum at the bottom of my purse. My rescuer also refuses my check. He demands cash up front instead. I offer the remaining cake as partial payment, but "Happy Birth" doesn't appeal to him either.

A warrior is on her knees before dawn. She eloquently prays for missionaries in far-off lands as well as for the lady next door. She covers international affairs, foreign heads of state, and the members of her city council. All before her first cup of coffee.

When the alarm shatters my sleep, my mind muddles through a thick fog. *Did I survive the night? I must have. Heaven would surely be cleaner than this bedroom.* An inkling of gratitude for my family, the stress, and even the mess might sneak up on me. I may hear myself mumbling, "Good morning, Lord, and thank you." Not eloquent, but better those my first words than, "Hey! Who took my hair dryer and didn't put it back?"

When a warrior's friend calls her with a concern, before her friend even gets the details out, the warrior says gently, "Let's pray about that, shall we?" And then she prays right there on the phone. Out loud! I pity the friends of wimps like me. A call like that becomes a mutual whining session about the tough stuff of life, with a promise to pray for each other. Later. When nobody can hear me. A promise I usually forget.

A warrior's prayers are a symphony; mine are advertising jingles.

"Lord, I deserve a break today!"
"Reach out, reach out and touch me, God."
"Can you hear me now? Can you hear me now?"

A warrior's prayer time is an elegant, intimate dinner for two; mine is a fast-food run. "I'll take a new heart, a new mind, and two orders of patience, Lord. And could I please have that to go!"

"Make time for appointments with God," the experts advise. Oh, sure! Exactly when would I be able to do that? Before the soccer game after the basketball practice between the ballet class and the Scout troop meeting? After my early morning meeting, between my midmorning meeting and my late-morning meeting? When I'm asleep maybe?

"Pray for your family while you're cooking." Hmm. That would be while the Mac-N-Cheez-to-Go heats in the microwave. I hope my family doesn't have any problems that can't be solved in four minutes or less.

"Pray while you're folding laundry," I've heard. If I'm praying, who's going to yell at the kids, demanding to know who threw the red shirt in with the—now pink—whites? How am I going to grumble about the missing socks if I'm busy talking to God?

The Bible says, "Pray without ceasing"? Is the Bible joking? In this day and age? Run, clean, fuss, fume, and work without ceasing, yes. Organize, stress, agonize, groan, and whine without ceasing, yes. But *pray* without ceasing? Who has time for *that*? Between the family's stuff and my countless other jobs, I'm Jonah in the whale of busyness.

Oh, there have been rare moments I've spent with God. Rare times when the children were all off at camp, when I was sick in bed, when my back was out, or when I was just too pooped to do another thing—then I could manage those appointments. Then it was like a spiritual teeth cleaning. A whole lot of uncomfortable scraping, grinding, and flossing just to get rid of the plaque of my life. And that slick, clean feeling afterward sure doesn't last long.

Who wants to go to the dentist every day?

So I'm a prayer wimp. I have trouble being focused enough, disciplined enough, organized enough—or whatever it is they are—to be a prayer warrior. I don't seem to have the calling, the blessing, the power—or whatever it is they have—to do the job. I'm not Wonder Woman, not a warrior, when it comes to praying. I'm a wimp.

What can I do? Where can I go for help? Is there a twelve-step program for people like me? A place where I could stand before a bunch of strangers and confess, "My name is Mary, and I am a prayer wimp." Murmurs of understanding would assure me I'm not alone. No one would throw rocks.

It's hard to know what to do. It's hard to find a prayer warrior who will give me any advice. I've asked friends at church, "Know any prayer warriors?" They've given me other people's names. Prayer warriors, I've discovered, don't seem to realize who they are. Anytime I've approached one and asked, "Can you teach me how to be a prayer warrior like you are?" they've responded, "Ha! Me? A prayer warrior? No way!"

Prayer warriors often insist they too are wimps. One told me, "We're all just raw recruits in God's army." She suggested that prayer might not be about who *we* are at all but about who God is. Then she said God will teach us to pray if we ask him. If that's the case, then the twelve-step plan for recovering wimps would be simple:

Step 1: Say, "Lord, teach me to pray."
Step 2: Be quiet and listen.
Steps 3–12: Repeat steps 1 and 2 until you hear differently.

It sounds simple enough, even for a wimp like me.

> You who seek God, may your hearts live!
> —Psalm 69:32

points to ponder

1. How busy are you? How does your busyness compare to that of women in previous generations? Are we busier today, yes or no? Defend your answer.

2. What challenges in life turn you into a wimp? When are you a warrior?

3. Describe the current state of your prayer life. What changes would you like to see?

is it God or Charlton Heston?

It's no surprise that I have trouble sitting quietly and listening to God. Some people seem to have a gift for listening. I do not. When a friend is pouring out her heart to me, it's hard for me to just listen. I'm usually thinking about what I'm going to say back to her, the good advice I'll offer that will, I am sure, be just what she needs to hear to solve her problem. I can't wait until it's my turn to talk.

But one cool autumn day (after a friend told me I needed to), I decided to try to tune in to God's voice. I sat down in a chair at the kitchen table, facing the back deck and the woods, the most peaceful, least distracting view in the house. I folded my hands together on the table in front of me.

"Okay, God, here I am," I said, as if he needed me to tell him that. "I'm ready to listen." I waited. I heard nothing. I waited some more, straining to hear something, anything, that sounded like somebody else's voice. The furnace, in the basement right below the kitchen table, kicked on with a whoosh as the gas ignited. The furnace fan kicked into action. The metal miniblinds rattled against the kitchen window frame as the forced air rose from the floor vent. I heard all that, but nothing that sounded like God.

"I'm listening, Lord," I said again and inhaled deeply. I looked out the window again. Squinted actually. The window badly needed washing. The trees in the woods had begun to change color. I'd need to rake soon. And I knew I should divide some of my hostas and spread them out to more spots. The woodpile needed restacking, and we hadn't put the sealer coat on the deck yet.

So much to do. I closed my eyes and held my breath to try to focus my mind. I felt a faint *ka-swish, ka-swish* in my carotid artery and in my ears. My own pulse. I exhaled loudly, cleared my throat, wiggled into a more comfy position, and tried again.

"Lord, I'm listening." Silence. A chipmunk scrambled along the deck railing, stopping at the black-oil sunflower seed feeder to fill his cheeks. He was busy with his to-do list. Shouldn't I be? The fall cleaning wasn't done. A pot of soup would be good for dinner. My wool coat needed dry cleaning. Where had I packed the mittens and scarves the previous spring? We'd need them soon. The car needed a seasonal tune-up. So did I.

"Honestly!" I said aloud in disgust. I shook my head to clear my brain and closed my eyes. "I'm here, Lord. I'm listening."

Just then a Bible verse popped into my head. "Be still, and know that I am God." I'd read that verse a bunch of times. I even knew where it was in the Bible. Psalm 46:10. I knew the verse. I'd sung the song. I wondered, *Is this how God speaks, in my head, sounding just like me?* The thought had just come to mind. Was it God?

What does God sound like when he speaks to you? I don't really know what I was expecting to hear. Maybe I was expecting something more booming and majestic, a voice like thunder. Maybe I was expecting Charlton Heston.

It's hard to know what God will sound like, or if we should even be hearing him. Some people who've claimed to hear his voice have gotten into trouble. Joan of Arc, for instance. Some people say prayer is a supernatural conversation that involves speaking and listening, which means that God is going to say something to you. Others call it "lunacy" when people hear God talking. But God spoke to people in the Bible all the time. I'd read about the prophet Elijah's experience with hearing the voice of God.

Do you know the story? It's detailed in 1 Kings 19:1–13, but I'll sum it up here. Elijah was pooped out. God had been working him pretty hard in the idol-worshiping land of King Ahab. Elijah cleaned house, and that got him in trouble with Ahab's wicked wife, Jezebel. They don't come much wickeder than Jezebel. Elijah ran for his life.

He ended up in a cave, and God asked him a question: "What are you doing here, Elijah?" Then God told him to step outside the cave, on the mountain, "in the presence of the LORD, for the LORD is about to pass by." Not only was God speaking to Elijah, but God was about to make a physical appearance.

It seems Elijah stayed in the cave as "a great and powerful wind tore the mountains apart and shattered the rocks before the LORD." We who live in tornado country can't help but shudder at that. We too stay in our caves when that kind of stuff is going on outside.

"But the LORD was not in the wind. After the wind there was an earthquake." That would have gotten my attention, having lived in southern California. The earth moving is quite the little attention-getter!

The story continues. "But the LORD was not in the earthquake. After the earthquake came a fire." Poor Elijah, stuck at the intersection of Catastrophe Avenue and Disaster Drive.

"But the LORD was not in the fire." How often I've seen God in creation, in natural phenomena. I've glimpsed his glory in a sunset. I've sensed his strength in a storm. But on that day, on that mountain, God wasn't using any of those things to communicate with Elijah.

"And after the fire came a gentle whisper." A gentle whisper. A small voice. When Elijah heard it, he must have gathered his courage, for "he pulled his cloak over his face and went out and stood at the mouth of the cave."

The voice repeated the earlier question. "What are you doing here, Elijah?"

Elijah heard the gentle whisper of God. I'm amazed that he could hear anything. I would have still been screaming in fear after the wind, earthquake, and fire. But Elijah heard. He heard the gentle whisper of God.

Is this how God speaks? No Charlton Heston–Moses voice, no megaphones or loudspeakers, but a gentle whisper?

No wonder it's hard to hear God's voice in the clamor of life, over the noise pollution of television and radio. It's hard to be still enough to hear gentle whispers when you are inundated by the ceaseless demands of children, spouse, friends, and the ringing telephone. The requests to serve on the committee, command the troop, coach the team, chauffeur the group, call the parents, and yes, even to pray for others.

So many pressing demands. So little time. A committee report for this afternoon's meeting must be done *before* the meeting, not tomorrow. Tonight's dinner must be ready for *tonight*, not tomorrow. A diaper that needs changing needs changing *now*, not tomorrow.

"Be still," God tells me. "Tune out the demands for a moment. Tune out the clamor." How can I do that? Maybe I can sneak off into a corner when the family is away. I might be able to hole up in a locked room when they're home. Perhaps I can let my calls go to voicemail. (Did you know you can turn off the ringer on your telephone? Have you ever actually turned it off? Try it; you'll like it!)

I can ignore the magazines and newspapers and decline to answer the doorbell. I can turn off the television, the radio, and the music and set aside today's to-do list. I can ignore my inner nag and her list of "shoulds" and "have tos." I can set it all aside, for a moment. Can you? Right now?

"What are you doing here, Elijah?" the Lord asked. I sense him asking me the same question. What am I doing here, with my life, with my days, with my moments? What are you doing here, with your life, your days, your moments?

How do we find the time to listen to God when the calendar is packed full with other things? How can we listen to God when we don't allow any time in our day for quiet reflection?

"Be *still*, and know that I am God," he says.

Right now, wherever you are, take a deep breath. Hold it a moment. Exhale slowly. For some of us, this is the first deep breath we've taken since 1985. Some of us have just experienced what it is to "be still" for the first time.

"Be still, and *know* that I am God." Who is this God anyway? Do I know? Am I seeking to know the God who is, or the God I want him to be? Do I want God to be like the broom in the closet—used to clean up the messes I've made and then set aside when things are tidied up? Do I want God to be my safe harbor in the storms of life, when my little ship is being tossed on the angry seas, but far from my mind when the waters are calm? Do I want God to be a benign, opinion-less "force" available to help me go where *I* want to go, to advance *my* agenda, to achieve *my* idea of success?

Who is God?

"Be still, and know . . ." Do I *want* to know the God who is Sovereign Lord of the universe, Creator of heaven and earth—my Creator? All-powerful God? He is the one who created me, and without his sustaining power in my life, I have nothing. I am nothing without God. Nothing.

Psalm 46:10 reads, in another Bible translation, "Cease striving and know that I am God" (NASB). To cease striving means to quit trying so hard. Stop struggling. Retreat from the battle. Stop working so hard. Resign the position. Lose the briefcase. Drop out of the rat race. Stop, drop everything, and be still.

"Cease striving." That sounds so good to me, so welcome. For a moment—this moment—I will sit quietly and let that idea sink in. I'll allow myself to be awed by the notion that God Almighty invites me to be still in his presence. I'll sit and let the wondrous truth settle over me—that the Sovereign Lord of all creation invites me to know him in this life, to draw near to him on this day, to bask in his love for this moment.

"Come with me by yourselves to a quiet place and get some rest" (Mark 6:31). Listen to him gently whisper the invitation to you too: "Come with me to a quiet place. Get some rest."

Come. Rest. Be still and know.

> He leads me beside quiet waters,
> he restores my soul.
>   —Psalm 23:2–3

points to ponder

1. What makes a good listener? Are you a good listener? How can you improve? Who needs you to listen to them today?

2. Think about your to-do list for a moment. Identify one thing you can dump or delegate right now. Do it, and then celebrate with a cup of hot chocolate with marshmallows or with something else wonderful. Congratulations!

3. "Come with me by yourselves to a quiet place and get some rest." How and when will you answer God's invitation?

the worst of mornings

Come with me back in time to a morning long ago, to Minneapolis, to a little house in the big city. It was the worst of mornings. I was trying to get six-year-old Alex ready for school, three-year-old Katy and baby Betsy ready to take to the sitter, and myself, their single mother, ready to go to work.

The day had not started well. The alarm blasted me awake at 5:30 a.m. as usual, and I had a headache. I'd been up late the night before, finishing the laundry and trying to get some other housework done. I had three kids and only two hands.

I took a couple of aspirin and got dressed for the office. Nothing fit right. I'd been a stay-at-home mother for years. Lots of at-home moms manage to maintain their sense of style. I never did, and I had the wardrobe to prove it. Maternity clothes, jeans, and sweatshirts were my mainstays. My navy hooded sweatshirt and my jeans were *de rigueur* for the neighborhood coffee gatherings, the bowling league, and the park programs, but the workplace demanded a fashion sense I'd lost touch with. I'd been having "casual Friday" long before it became a workplace fad. But then I also had casual Monday through casual Thursday. Casual decade, actually.

When I went back to work outside the home, I resurrected my "good" clothes from the back of my closet. So what if my pant legs were too wide and my skirts too long to be in style? I wasn't about to buy new clothes until I had a chance to lose some of the baby fat that insulated my hindquarters. So that morning I put on the skirt and blouse that of all my outfits, looked the least like sausage casings. Now I had to get the children ready. If we hurried, I could get to work on time.

I woke Alex and laid out the last clean shirt he had, dusted off his jeans from the day before, and extricated his shoes from the pile of I-didn't-want-to-know-what under his bed. While he dressed, I changed the baby and woke Katy. We all hustled into the kitchen, where I whipped up some oatmeal.

Alex took his bowl and headed to the living room to spend quality time with his cartoon friends. With my left hand, I tried to keep Betsy's oatmeal in her bowl; she was determined to mousse her hair with it. With a hairbrush in my right hand, I began to detangle Katy's long blond hair. Multitasking at its finest.

The brush stuck. I lifted Katy's long locks from the side of her head to see what the problem was.

"Aack!" I screamed. A *huge* glob of purple bubble gum was firmly wadded in Katy's hair. She'd obviously gone to bed with gum in her mouth. Just another of the million little details I felt guilty about missing.

"Aack!" Betsy echoed, laughing as she grabbed a gob of oatmeal in her pudgy little fist and heaved it in my direction. I tried to jump out of the way. It hit my shoe. The kid had quite an arm. (She would, years later, win the fifth-grade girls' softball pitch contest. But that's another story.)

"No!" I scolded her. She grinned and reached into the bowl to reload. I grabbed the bowl away from her. She sat smearing her hands into her hair, repeating, "Aack! Aack! Aack!"

"Girls, I don't have time for this! What am I going to do with this gum wad?" Panic churned my stomach, for this was before the days of the do-it-yourself network, before the "You Got a Problem? We've Got a Guru!" information age. I couldn't run to my computer and Google "gum wad" and find a hundred websites offering everything from the history of chewing gum (Did the inventors really get the idea from watching cows chew their cud, like my mother said?) to Bazooka Joe's biography. (Why *is* his turtleneck covering his mouth? Is there gum stuck on his lip?)

Back then we didn't have all those resources that offer a ready answer for every possible homemaking dilemma. We had to blunder along, figuring out solutions as we went. I racked my brain. Hadn't I just read something about removing bubble gum? Was it in *Woman's Day*? Was it a hint from Heloise? Or had I heard it on the streets?

"Aha!" I shouted. "Peanut butter!" Betsy looked at me, interested.

"Mo'?" She wanted more to eat. Of course. She'd used her oatmeal as hair mousse and ammunition.

"Sorry, baby. You'll have to wait," I said. Hoping that peanut butter would work, I grabbed the jar of cheapo-store-brand extra chunky from the kitchen cupboard, tucked a daughter under each arm, and flew into the bathroom. I ran water into the tub, plopped the girls in, and started working the peanut butter into the gum.

The purple goo resisted at first, then started to dissolve. Sweet victory was mine! With a fine comb, I carefully lifted the disintegrating chunks from Katy's hair. I shampooed and scrubbed both girls, dried them off, dressed them, and parked them by the front door. "Sit! Stay!" I commanded. They looked at me with puppy eyes.

I turned to Alex. "Come!" We had only a few minutes to get out the door. I finger-combed his hair, straightened his shirt, retied his shoes, spit-washed his face (all mothers know this technique), and the four of us hustled across the street to the neighbors' house. Alex would wait there with their son, his best friend, for the school bus.

After kissing Alex goodbye, I hurried back home with the girls, locked up our house, packed them into the car, and sped the six blocks to the babysitter's house. I dropped the girls off, zoomed to the bus stop, parked my car, jumped on the packed bus, jockeyed for position near the back door, grabbed an overhead bar, and dangled there for the half-hour ride into the city.

My mind reeled. *Did I turn off the coffeepot? Did Alex have lunch money? Did I remember to send his permission slip for the field trip? Did I give Katy her medication this morning?* (She had chronic ear infections.) *Did I remember to pack Betsy's blanket for the sitter?* (She couldn't sleep without it—Betsy, not the sitter.) *Is there enough milk at home for supper, or do I need to stop at the store after work? What are we having for supper anyway? Am I coming down with something? I feel a little dizzy.*

Once downtown, I hustled the three blocks to our office building, rushed inside to my desk, and plopped myself down—a mere fifteen minutes late—to begin my day at "work." Ha! *What a woman!*

The office was actually my place of rest. Life was so very, very hectic as a single working mother. Spending my day with grown-ups, who hardly ever got bubble gum in their hair, was a relief. Almost like a vacation. Almost.

The day would end with the morning scenario replayed in reverse. On the bus ride home I'd be wondering, *Did I do that report well enough? Was the boss a little upset or was I imagining things? Did Alex have a good day? Is tonight the open house at his school or is that next week? Or was that last week? Is Katy's ear going to be okay? Do I have anything clean to wear to work tomorrow? Did we have milk in the refrigerator when I left this morning? What am I making for dinner tonight? I hope the kids go to bed early. I think I am coming down with something.*

All mothers are "working" mothers. There is no question about that. But single working mothers hold down at least two full-time jobs, sometimes more. Becoming a single mother gave me increased appreciation for the value of that other parent. A second pair of hands to tie shoes and wipe noses. A relief pitcher for those moments when you're worn out in the ninth inning. Someone who can offer a second opinion, an opinion expressed (usually) without whining or a temper tantrum. Another lap. Another voice to read bedtime stories. No question about it, parenting is a full-time, two grown-up job. It's definitely not for the faint of heart.

But there I was, not by choice, doing it on my own. Where was peace during that hectic time? Where was time to rest, relax, and recharge? Nowhere. Those days were filled with guilt, frustration, and endless work. Those days were short on fun, rest, and quiet.

Have you "been there, done that"? Did you feel—or maybe feel today—what I felt? Weary, worried, and whipped. The time-management experts and the parenting pros told me I needed to be sure to include some "me time" in my day. I'd be a better mother, they assured me. Right. Maybe I could squeeze some me time in between my massage appointment and my pedicure. Right after my elephant's flying lesson.

Me time was a dream for a distant someday. Even a bathroom break was interrupted by a little hand knocking on the door. "Mommy? Are you in there?" They were too young to be left alone, but a few times I stepped outside and stood looking up into the forty-foot pine tree in the front yard. I wondered if the highest branches would hold my weight. I didn't dare risk it with my insulated hindquarters.

Where was solitude? Where was sanity? I didn't have time for anything else after work, hugs, cooking, and what passed for housekeeping—scraping the dried and crusty oatmeal off the kitchen floor; washing, drying, sorting, and folding a hundred changes of clothes a week (two of them mine); removing the recongealed bubble gum from the bathtub drain.

There may have been a moment of peace and quiet in the evening after the children were changed, their teeth brushed, their stories read, their prayers said, but most nights I was too exhausted to notice as I fell into bed. Each day ran into the next with grinding regularity and the mind-numbing reality of too much to do and too little time. I was living at a deficit— a physical, emotional, and spiritual deficit.

There was just no time anywhere for anything other than the demands of the day. There are those seasons in life when we are busy. We're busy because we're doing something incredibly important—solo parenting small children or providing primary care to an ailing loved one, for instance—and our time and energy must be given fully to the job at hand. That's just the way it is. We're busy because we have to be busy. And day after day, we simply get up and do it again, because we have to.

Two decades have passed since the "worst of mornings," but I remember it well. I remember collapsing into bed at night, sometimes crying myself to sleep. More often, I was simply just too tired to cry, too tired to think.

My prayers were simple: "Help!" and "Yikes!" If I prayed more than that, my requests revolved around immediate concerns. No praying for the events of the world. No praying for much of anything or anyone outside the walls of my home. I was powerless to pray for anything but my own needs. Powerless to do anything more than the minimum daily requirements. Powerless to cope, but for the grace of God.

My prayers were simple but from the heart—my broken heart.

Lord, protect Alex at school today. Bring him home safely.

Lord, please heal Katy's ear infection.

Lord, keep Betsy well.

Lord, keep the car running.

Dear God, help me to be enough mother for these children. Give me strength for tomorrow . . . and the next day . . . and the next.

> Show me your ways, O LORD,
>   teach me your paths;
> guide me in your truth and teach me,
>   for you are God my Savior,
>   and my hope is in you all day long.
> —Psalm 25:4–5

points to ponder

1. Describe the most hectic season in your life. How did you manage? Who helped you get through it? Or maybe you are in that season now. How are you coping? What changes do you need to make?

2. Describe your favorite quiet place. What's wonderful about it?

3. What is the prayer concern that weighs heaviest on your heart right now? Share it with God.

Bingo was his name-oh!

Terry and I married a few years after that "worst of mornings." We lived in California, and every other weekend, we were the Brady Bunch. His three and my three (ages four to thirteen) and Terry and me—crammed into the old Buick, rolling down the freeways. Every car ride was accompanied by the kids' sing-along tape.

We crooned along to "Buffalo Gals" and "Oh, Susanna." We sang about the plight of "The Old Lady Who Swallowed a Fly." None of us knew why she swallowed that fly either.

We sang each verse of one particular favorite softer and softer until the final verse, which we mouthed silently until the end, when all eight of our voices screamed out, "John Jacob Jingleheimer Schmitt!" We belted out the tale of the farmer who had the dog named B-I-N-G-O. Yes, Bingo was his name. Oh. Over and over, ride after ride. The saints went marching in, and Yankee Doodle was dandy in those days.

Not too long ago Terry and I made a holiday trip with Katy and Lizz (the baby formerly known as Betsy) in the back seat of the car. They were both in their twenties, but just for old times' sake, they'd been acting, for fifty miles or more, like five-year-olds.

"Mom! She's *looking* at me! Make her *stop!*" Katy demanded.

"But Mom, she's hogging the back seat. Make her *move!*" Lizz said, giving her older sister a shove. Then together they whined, "Are we *there* yet?" and dissolved into giggles. Suddenly they both let out a shriek as they started a tickle fight.

"Don't make me stop this car!" Terry threatened in mock anger. We'd had enough nonsense. It was time for the big guns. I reached into the glove compartment and pulled out the secret weapon I'd stashed there for just such an emergency.

"I've got the tape!" I hollered, waving the familiar yellow cassette over my head.

"No, please! Not the tape! We'll be good!" The girls begged for mercy, but I just gave a sinister laugh.

"Ha! Too late!" With a dramatic flourish, I pushed the cassette into the player and cranked up the volume. The girls groaned as Terry and I launched at the top of our lungs into excruciatingly off-key renditions of the old songs.

"Had an old dog, and his name was Bl-u-u-u-ue," we howled. From there we crooned the virtues of our "Darling Clementine." We twanged our way, sourly, through "Camptown Races." I thought our "doo-dahs" were particularly inspired.

As we reminded ourselves (as if we could ever forget) that "Bingo was his name-oh!" I looked back. Both girls had their fingers jammed into their ears and their eyes squeezed shut.

"Make it stop! Make it stop!" they moaned, writhing on the back seat. I smiled. Revenge was sweet.

I've always loved music. I would lie in bed in the dark as a child, singing myself to sleep with every song I knew. When

I was in third grade, I would sing all the songs I'd learned in school, beginning with the first-grade songs. "My little red wagon is lots of fun; it runs as well as a Ford. Along on the sidewalk, we roll and run. Look out for us all aboard!" I sang through "Polly Wolly Doodle" and "Waltzing Matilda." I sang patriotic songs and silly songs. Music had the power, I discovered, to soothe the savage eight-year-old. I sang myself to sleep, night after night.

My parents loved singing too. I can still hear them harmonizing in the front seat of the car as we rode along, singing the songs of their youth. "You must remember this . . . ," "I'll be loving you . . . always," and "I'll be looking at the moon, but I'll be seeing you."

I heard a man on NPR one night not too long ago as I drove home from a meeting. His voice soft in the dark car, he described the way his mother, while she was going through a divorce, played the saddest songs over and over. "Wallowing songs," he called them. He confessed that later in life he too had his own brokenhearted songs. He'd come to understand the healing power of sad songs, healing because the artist is singing the song right from your own heart.

Has your heart ever been broken? Do you have any "wallowing songs"?

My father loved music and he loved the piano. When I was five, my mother wrote numbers on the keys of the old upright Kimball that was a fixture in our apartment living room. She showed me how to play "Twinkle, Twinkle, Little Star" by the numbers. I was hooked.

When I was ten, I carved my initials in the piano's mahogany front, staking my claim. By the time I was fifteen, I could do a fair job playing some popular pieces and a few simple—very simple—classical arrangements. My father often asked me to play for him. As I played songs from *West Side Story*, he sat in his big brown velveteen armchair, eyes closed, resting his head against the chair's high back, fingers tapping the worn upholstery.

Later, as he got sicker with lung cancer, our concert fare turned melancholy. He sat in the chair, with his ever-present Camel, requesting one sad song after another. "Dear Heart" was a favorite. By the following January, he'd quit smoking. He'd sit in the chair, his burgundy cardigan hanging loose on his thinning frame. His false teeth no longer fit in his mouth, so he had stopped wearing them. His sunken cheeks made his chin more prominent.

"Lyndon Johnson. That's who I look like," he said, without laughing. I played "September Song" for him.

By March the lump on his chest was visible through his shirts, his cough dry and nearly constant. He sat for long hours, smaller then in the brown chair, trying to keep breathing. He asked me to play "Stranger on the Shore."

Sometimes he'd ask me to softly play "How Great Thou Art," "The Old Rugged Cross," "Rock of Ages."

Sometimes he'd tell me to stop. Listening was too much work. I was almost seventeen.

At my father's funeral, one of his friends played part of Dvořák's *New World Symphony* on the organ. Someone had put words to Dvořák's melody: "Going home . . . going home . . ." That movement from *New World* is one of my wallowing songs. There is a time to mourn, the Bible says. A time to be sad, to cry, to grieve. Sad songs help us do that.

Other songs affect me differently. Roberta Flack singing "Killing Me Softly" takes me to Washington, D.C., on vacation, visiting my girlfriend Cary. We're twenty-one, laughing, talking, and hanging out there in her apartment in this city of power and politics. Roberta Flack, Cary, and me. Young. Dreaming. Hopeful.

I hear "Bye, Bye, Miss American Pie" and I'm in the living room of a rented apartment above a liquor store in Highland Falls, New York. The apartment walls are painted a high-gloss orange, and the trim is all black—a Halloween room, courtesy of the previous tenants. I live there with my first husband, who is a military policeman in the army, stationed at West Point. The Vietnam War rages half a world away, but here we are safe. Here we are in love. The song reminds me.

I hear "Total Eclipse of the Heart" and it's thirteen years later and I'm divorced. Heartbroken. No longer falling in love, just falling apart, like the song says: "Nothing I can do. A total eclipse of the heart." The artist felt what I was feeling. She sang my pain. Another wallowing song.

The opening notes of "Heard It through the Grapevine" instantly put me in the passenger seat of that classic dark burgundy Buick Riviera of Terry's, cruising down the freeway. He's put the sound track from *The Big Chill* in the tape player. He looks at me and smiles. I look at him—this man who would become my second, and last, husband—and I realize for the first time that I love him.

We share a past in this "golden oldies" music, a past we didn't share with each other. We hope; we dream of a future together. I fell in love to the opening bass notes of that song—which is, ironically, about the end of love, not the beginning. But that doesn't matter, because I hear those notes today and I am back in that old Riviera, falling in love again.

In the Bible, the prophet Jonah talked about singing while he was in the belly of the great fish. "But I, with a song of thanksgiving, will sacrifice to you. What I have vowed I will make good. Salvation comes from the LORD" (Jonah 2:9).

Jonah prepared his song of thanksgiving in the depths of his trouble.

At times the waters of change or pain wash over us, threatening to drown us, to carry us deeper and deeper into the cold, dark water of despair. We cry out, like the psalmist (the songwriters of the Bible) who cried: "Save me, O God, for the waters have come up to my neck. I sink in the miry depths, where there is no foothold. I have come into the deep waters; the floods engulf me. . . . Rescue me from the mire, do not let me sink. . . . Do not let the floodwaters engulf me or the depths swallow me up" (Psalm 69:1–2, 14–15).

When life's sorrows swallow you up, can you sing thanksgiving to God? Can you sing from the belly of the whale?

There is a song based on Lamentations 3:22–23: "Because of the LORD's great love we are not consumed, for his compassions never fail. They are new every morning; great is your faithfulness." I hear that song and I am in the car, driving to work on a sunny fall morning in Southern California. I see students walking toward the junior high school. My son Alex is not among them. He is supposed to be there but has chosen to live this school year with his father back in Minnesota instead.

I cry as I drive, missing him. Then the Lamentations song comes to mind, and I sing this comfort from God. Sooner or later all the people I love will move away from me, in one way or another. But through it all, the song reminds me, God's great love remains steadfast. His compassion toward me is renewed every morning. Love, strength, mercy, grace— all new every morning, sufficient for the day. I sing—through tears, yes, but I sing.

My favorite song must be "Amazing Grace." I hear it and I'm a young mother of two. I'm driving down the street in our old neighborhood, just having dropped Alex off at the preschool summer program at the local park. The radio is on and I hear "Amazing Grace," not the words, just the melody. This is an instrumental rendition, all brass and bass. *Amazing grace, how sweet the sound.*

The clarion tones are the trumpet call of God to my heart. *I once was lost, but now am found.* I know, listening, that I am lost. I've drifted away from God. Twelve years after my father's death, I'm still mad at God for letting it happen. I'm trying to find my own way through the pain, but I've gotten lost somehow.

I hear a soft voice say, "All you have to do is ask." I know what that means. I've heard it before. From the Book Nook sisters. From my Christian sister-in-law, Joanne. All I have to do is ask, and God will comfort and console me. Just ask, and God will forgive my rebellion and anger. Just ask, and God will welcome me back into his arms, turn my life around again, and heal my heart.

All I have to do is ask. The song assures me that God still loves me, after all my rejecting him, rebelling against him, and refusing his love. He still loves me. I listen to the melody. I know the words. I know that I "was blind, but now I see."

"Okay, Lord. I'm asking," I say softly in surrender. French horn and trombone resonate with God's amazing grace as he changes my life once more, in an instant.

I hear the song today and I remember. I am his. I am his.

> By day the LORD directs his love,
> at night his song is with me—
> a prayer to the God of my life.
> —Psalm 42:8

points to ponder

1. What's your favorite song and why? What memories do you associate with particular songs? Reconnect this week with your favorite music. Get comfy and spend some time just listening. Enjoy!

2. Are there certain songs or a style of music you just can't stand to listen to? Why not? What kind of sacred music do you enjoy? Do you prefer traditional hymns or contemporary compositions? Why?

3. Are there particular songs that make you feel closer to God? What about them touches you? Is it the words? The images? The melody? Enjoy some of those songs this week. (If you don't have any such favorites, ask a friend what her favorites are. Ask her to share them with you.)

beware the ides of march

One March 15th, Terry and I sat at breakfast trying to recall why that date, "the ides of March," was significant. In our foggy recollection (we were sharing a brain that morning), we sensed it had something to do with Shakespeare. Was it the day Mrs. Macbeth washed her hands? Was it Romeo and Juliet's anniversary? Was Julius Caesar involved? Yes, we agreed. March 15th had something to do with Caesar.

We pursued a conversational rabbit trail for a while, wondering how Caesar salad got its name. Back to the subject at hand, we decided we had to have an answer. I ran to my office and returned to the kitchen with our *Dictionary of Cultural Literacy*.

Digging into that dictionary (actually an encyclopedia and dictionary combined), we were amazed to discover how many connections we had to Julius Caesar—besides salad and C-sections. Caesar crossed the Rubicon. We still refer to making irrevocable decisions as "crossing the Rubicon."

After a campaign in Asia, Caesar reported to the senate, "Veni, vidi, vici," which is Latin for "I came, I saw, I conquered."

I had a T-shirt once that said VENI, VIDI, VISA, which was translated on the shirt: I CAME, I SAW, I BOUGHT. I'll bet Mrs. Caesar had a shirt just like it.

"Beware the ides of March," we learned, was a fortune-teller's warning to Caesar in Shakespeare's *Julius Caesar*. Caesar was assassinated on March 15th. It's amazing how much vitally important information a person can pick up between bites of Bran Flakes.

In Shakespeare's play, Caesar saw a fortune-teller. And the fortune-teller's prediction proved true. When I was in sixth grade, my mother went to a parent-teacher conference, and my teacher, Mr. Renard, had dire predictions for my future. He predicted that I'd never make it through junior high. Can you imagine that? What a terrible thing to say to somebody's mommy! His reason for my future failure? I never contributed to class discussions. Ever.

The idea of actually raising my hand—an embarrassingly huge paw hanging there at the end of my scrawny little arm—and volunteering an answer filled me with terrible trepidation. I could—perish the thought—be wrong!

The fear of being called on was even worse. My heart pounding, my palms sweating, I knew that if my name was called, my brain would cease functioning, my throat would close, and my neck and face would burn red, as if I'd caught fire. So I kept a low profile, skulking down behind the boy in front of me and straightening my pencils while Mr. Renard scouted the room for his next victim.

I'd taken to heart what my father always said: "It's better to say nothing and let people think you're a fool than to open your mouth and dispel all doubt." My fear of being wrong, of looking foolish, kept me mum in class.

I bore the shame of a scarlet N, for Needs Improvement, on my report card under the category Contributes to Class Discussion. The N for "failure" didn't motivate me; it made me even more self-conscious. Mr. Renard—a teacher and therefore always right—had envisioned my future, examined my tea leaves, read my horoscope, and checked with the stars. I was doomed.

I was shy, quiet, and thoughtful. I preferred to sit back and take in all that was going on around me, listening to comments and ideas and forming my own impressions. I was observant, storing up material for later (this chapter, for instance).

I absorbed things. The dusty smell of the classroom, with a faint scent of green soap. The way the television teacher looked on the fuzzy black-and-white set our teacher rolled into the classroom for social studies. The man on the little screen stood stiffly in his black suit and tie; I could tell he didn't like talking to kids, even over the television. Sometimes we listened to science programs on the classroom radio. What a bore—science without visual aids. No flashes, no smoke, no smells, no explosions. Just a disembodied voice droning on and on.

I was a thinker, not a talker. An observer, not a participant. So the teacher predicted failure for me. However, I went on to observe my way through junior high, through high school, and through four years of college, without ever *once* contributing to a class discussion. After I'd received my teaching degree, I was working one day at a school, and there, in the teacher's lounge, sat Mr. Renard.

Oh, there are those sweet moments in life, aren't there?

I reminded him who I was. I reminded him how he had predicted my failure. He pretended not to remember. "I'm here for your job," I said. He laughed. He thought I was kidding.

Mr. Renard thought he knew what my future held, but Mr. Renard was wrong about me. I heard so many messages as I was growing up that the odds were against my having any kind of success in life. I was from an alcoholic home, and therefore, "they" said, I was forever a "child of an alcoholic who would grow up and become an adult child of an alcoholic." I'd have a propensity, they said, to become an alcoholic myself, never free from its curse, scarred forever. This, they said, would define me.

We lived in a poor neighborhood. When I was in college, children from my neighborhood were the target of suburban do-gooders who came to save them from an environment described as "culturally deprived." One of my college classmates signed up to work in my neighborhood one summer, helping the "deprived" children get some culture. As I left my house one day, I saw her herding a group of her charges in the direction of the local park. She saw me. "What are *you* doing here?" she asked, startled.

"I *live* here," I explained. The color drained from her face. She'd never thought of me as culturally deprived, I guess. My secret was out.

Deprived of culture? Ha! The do-gooders just didn't understand. Maybe the music didn't blast at all hours in their neighborhoods. Maybe garages weren't torched for entertainment on Friday nights where the do-gooders lived. Maybe they'd never seen the National Guard on their corner, restoring the neighborhood peace. They acted like those were bad things.

We weren't *deprived* of culture. Ours was just a *different* culture. The buzzword was eventually changed to "culturally disadvantaged." (Thank you. That's *so* much better!) Semantics aside, the "odds were agin' me." I was at least culturally disadvantaged, if not downright deprived, at the low end of the totem pole, behind the eight ball, born on the wrong side of the tracks, down in the boondocks. I was an inner-city girl with few prospects and limited possibilities. Statistics predicted a dismal future. But the statistics were wrong about me.

Years later, after I'd been a teacher, divorced, remarried, and returned to college for a business degree, I decided I wanted to become a stockbroker. I'd been working as an assistant to several brokers and wanted to become one myself. I applied for the job with our firm and was granted an interview at the head office in downtown Los Angeles. I dressed for the interview in my new suit with my "girl" tie. (It was the 1980s. Women who wanted to "play with the boys" had to look like boys. Those were the rules.)

I arrived at the interview on the thirty-second floor of a skyscraper and was ushered into the office of the head of the firm's sales department. I sat in a little chair, in my little suit, facing a great big desk. Behind the great big desk sat a great big man. Behind the great big man was a great big window, and outside that window, the great big city of Los Angeles stretched for miles and miles. I never felt more intimidated in my life.

What am I doing here? I wondered. *Grandma must have felt exactly like this at Ellis Island when she got off the boat from Finland in 1906. Yah.* (You betcha, as we say around these parts.)

The man behind the desk started asking me questions. After a while he started talking down to me. He told me he thought I was a little naïve. He implied that I should just go back to where I came from and forget this particular dream.

I suppose he thought he knew me, thought he could tell what I was made of. But he was wrong about me. He didn't know I'd already heard the lies. I'd already been told over and over that I couldn't have what I thought I wanted, that I shouldn't bother to dream. I'd already been put down, shamed, and embarrassed. I'd already crashed into roadblocks and found detours. I'd already been run over by a steamroller or two. I'd already gotten up, more times than I could count, and continued on down the road. This was just a little bump.

Something changed during the interview. As we talked on, I explained who I was and where I'd been. I helped him see where I was going. I got the job.

Who's been predicting dire things for your future? What lies have you been listening to? Do you know the truth?

The teacher, the statisticians, the boss—they all thought they knew me, all thought they were right about my prospects and my future. But they were all wrong because they didn't know the truth. The truth is that God had other things in mind for me. God had plans to work things out for my wholeness.

He had a plan for wellness, a plan for healing, a plan for fulfillment. Not *in spite of* where I came from, but *because of* where I came from. God takes every hardship, every difficulty, every challenge—everything that others might call "curse"—and works it all together for my benefit. It's his promise. "And we know that in all things God works for the good of those who love him, who have been called according to his purpose" (Romans 8:28).

All things.

"They" thought they knew what was ahead for me. But they didn't know that God had other plans. Is someone predicting a dismal future for you? Pay no attention to the naysaying fortune-tellers. God has other plans for you too!

"For I know the plans I have for you," declares the LORD,
"plans to prosper you and not to harm you, plans to give you
hope and a future."

—Jeremiah 29:11

points to ponder

1. What hard knocks have you endured? What did they teach you?

2. Define "success" in terms of your career, your family life, and your personal life. In what areas of your life are you most successful and why?

3. What plans do you suppose God has for your future? What are you praying for? How are you preparing?

finding the
part three
way home

round peg, square hole

Stockbroker! I had arrived. I had achieved success at last. I had my own office, my own business cards, and a wonderful assistant. I had great new clothes and a great new image. My day planner, my briefcase, and my shoes were leather. Nice, soft leather. Need I say more?

Best of all, I had great dreams. I renewed my mind with all the self-improvement information I could lay my hands on. I studied how to think and grow rich, think like a winner, and think my way to the top. (I never stopped to think about the money all those authors were making by selling me their books.)

I boned up on goal setting and visualization. I imagined my future. I visualized my peers applauding my achievements as I accepted future accolades. I pictured my trophies on my credenza, my plaques on the wall, and my new car in the driveway. I'd accept, humbly, the thanks of the grateful recipients of my largesse. For I would not be selfish. Oh no, my wealth would be shared with the less fortunate. It was the least I could do.

How wonderful it was to be in this world, this sunny, upbeat, positive-thinking world. I'd spent enough time, I told myself, in the doldrums, in that gray twilight of under-achievement and settling for being less than all I could be. I had all the right stuff, and better still, the success gurus told me, I had *unlimited* potential for success! Vast storehouses of untapped genius!

I was only using *10 percent* of my brain, for cryin' out loud! I had an inner giant—a giant!—just waiting to be released. All I needed was some positive affirmation, some self-actual-ization, and some internal contemplation. I had a mother lode of possibility lurking just beneath my surface. All I had to do was mine it. The experts were ready to give me the right tools to do just that. I just had to want it badly enough.

Oh, I wanted it. I wanted it bad. *Real* bad. I developed dis-cipline. I learned how to smile and dial, cold-calling till the cows came home. I sacrificed. My family sacrificed. I went in to work early. I stayed at the office late. I memorized the mantras: Plan your work and work your plan. Anything works if you do. Eat the elephant one bite at a time.

But it was the dreams that kept me going. Dreams of mak-ing loads of money in a high-powered, fast-track kind of lifestyle—the polar opposite of my upbringing, where money was a necessary but elusive evil. In this job, money was wor-shiped for what it could provide. It was feared for what the loss of it could mean. We'd all heard the tales of the crash of 1929, when people leapt to their deaths from their office win-dows because they'd lost their money. (I was glad our offices were on street level.) Money was worshiped and money was feared. What power it had.

I loved my job, loved all the trappings that came with it. I loved it for a long time. Then came the day when I was about to get fired. By the time that day came, things had changed. I'd realized that the job was a great job, but it wasn't really me. I wasn't a numbers person; I was a words person. I could certainly handle the financial concepts and the math involved. I grasped the fundamentals of stocks and bonds, interest rates, and rates of return. But the job was primarily a sales job, and I was a lousy salesperson. I wasn't an out-front, aggressive go-getter of a girl. I hated calling strangers. I hated risking rejection.

I was, deep down, shy—an observer, an absorber, just like I'd been in sixth grade. I'd learned to pretend to be all I needed to be to fit the role. I was a chameleon. I looked great, but I was a fraud. The job I'd dreamed about, longed for, and worked for wasn't the right job for me. My heart just wasn't in it. I felt that one day my boss would walk in and fire me. And that day came.

I can still see the man walking through the lobby toward my glass-walled office. My stomach seized in a knot. I knew—I think you just *know*—that he was coming to fire me. I was right. We went to the conference room, and he started to say, "It's just not working out . . ."

It's horrible to be fired. Humiliating. Painful. For several years after that day, I had recurring visions of the boss, striding purposefully toward me. I remembered the look on his face and the knot in my stomach. Over time the experience took on monumental proportions in my mind. The memory became worse than the actual experience had been. Has that ever happened to you?

Then one day I decided to apply my highly developed imagination and visualization skills to taking the sting out of that memory. I began to picture the boss walking across that lobby wearing a clown outfit, with a big red nose. His feet are humungous, slapping the floor as he walks, and he hums a little tune. "Dum-tee dum-tee dum." He looks so ridiculous I can't help but laugh. You might want to try this with an unpleasant memory. It might help. Unless, of course, you are afraid of clowns.

Being fired is a terrible thing, but there is also something wonderful, something incredibly freeing, about it. I was in that job for all the wrong reasons. For the prestige I thought it gave me. For the nice clothes I got to wear. For the fancy client lunches and the rush of the gamble with clients who liked risky trading. The lure of wealth was like a drug.

The truth is it just wasn't me. The truth is the pursuit of money was not enough to satisfy me. The pursuit of money never is.

I pretended for a long time, and if I hadn't gotten fired, I would probably still be there today, trying to fit my round self into that square hole. (Like those hula hoops!) Getting fired forced me to reexamine my life and to think about my truest dreams—the dreams I'd been too afraid to dream. The dreams God had for me. Getting fired allowed me to let God's first choice for me—writing—become my first choice as well. That might never have happened if I hadn't been fired.

Getting fired set me free.

Disappointments can destroy us. Or our troubles can drive us to our knees and open our eyes, our ears, and our hearts to pay attention to God. God changes us, if we let him, through our challenges. The day the boss came to fire me, it turns out, was the best day I ever had on that job.

God used the firing as a tool to shape me. God is the Master Sculptor.

English clergyman G. H. Knight said, "It is only the eye of the sculptor that can see beforehand the finished statue in the rough marble block; but he does see it, and all the strokes of his tools are meant to bring out to the eyes of others what is already clear to his own. And the strokes of God's hand are only to produce the perfect beauty of the soul, and make that as visible to others as it now is to Himself. Nothing is more certain than that we will be perfectly satisfied with His work when we see it finished."

Knight asks, "Why should we not be satisfied now when He tells us what a glorious finish He will make, and leave to Him the choosing of the tools?"

How do I leave to God the choosing of the tools? How do I accept firing and failure, disease and disappointment? I was a welfare child who was allowed $1.25 a month for underwear. I knew what bulgur tastes like (not good); the government doled it out in ten-pound sacks to welfare families. Poverty shaped me. Would it shape me forever? My father's drinking scarred me. Would I be forever disfigured?

I was shy. "She'll never make it through junior high," my sixth-grade teacher had said. Would fear conceal the real me forever? "You'll never make it without me," my ex-husband said as he walked out the door. Was I abandoned forever? Later, divorce and bitterness twisted me into an angry and abusive parent. Was "sinner beyond redemption" my permanent label?

I raged against poverty and beat my fists against the pain of addiction's legacy. I kicked my heels on the floor when my first marriage fell apart. I cried in frustration over jobs ending. I screamed in protest when my children left the nest. I fought loneliness and aging like an enemy and sunk into despair and depression.

How difficult it is to let God choose the tools he'll use to shape me. If God is going to be working on me, I want him to use the soft tools—the quiet whisper, the gentle nudge. I don't want the chisel against my heart, the hammer ringing against the hard stone of my habits.

But who is the pot to argue with the potter? The prophet Jeremiah had this to say on the subject: "So I went down to the potter's house, and I saw him working at the wheel. But the pot he was shaping from the clay was marred in his hands; so the potter formed it into another pot, shaping it as seemed best to him." Jeremiah heard God's perspective then. "'Can I not do with you as this potter does?' declares the LORD. 'Like clay in the hand of the potter, so are you in my hand'" (Jeremiah 18:3–6).

Can God do with me as the potter does? Can he do the same with you? Certainly. Like clay in the hand of the potter, so are we in the hand of God.

And there is hope. "We have this treasure in jars of clay to show that this all-surpassing power is from God and not from us. We are hard pressed on every side, but not crushed; perplexed, but not in despair; persecuted, but not abandoned; struck down, but not destroyed" (2 Corinthians 4:7–9).

I must believe that through the kneading, the shaping, and the firing process that is at times perplexing and wearying— I must believe that God's every stroke is intentional. Purposeful. That his aim is to reveal to others what he himself already sees in me. That what he sees is something wonderful, something beautiful. Something he imagined when he first saw the clumsy slab, formless and dull, from which I will someday emerge.

What he sees is something so wonderful it is beyond my imagining. Grace upon grace, shining with truth and love and compassion. Glorious. Pure. Beautiful. The very image of Christ. Oh, the chasm that exists between what is and what he imagines will be! How grand his vision, how petty my thoughts. How immense his pleasure, how puny my praise. How amazing his artfulness, how crude my efforts.

It's hard to imagine that even now, as we yield to God, we "are being transformed into his likeness with ever-increasing glory, which comes from the Lord, who is the Spirit" (2 Corinthians 3:18). The image that God sees in us—the very image of Christ—will be revealed someday under the inspired crafting of the Divine Sculptor. That image—the hope of Christ—keeps me yielding to the Master's hand.

> Yet, O LORD, you are our Father.
> We are the clay, you are the potter;
> we are all the work of your hand.
> —Isaiah 64:8

points to ponder

1. Buy some modeling clay and sculpt something just for fun. (Try this in a group, with your family, or with friends.) If you have an interest in another art medium, try it. How do you feel about your creative efforts? Was the experience fun? Frustrating? Liberating? Embarrassing? Enlightening?

2. Make a list of the experiences that have shaped you into the person you are today. Which three experiences had the most dramatic impact? How so?

3. How has God been shaping you lately? Describe the process, the tools he is using, and how you're being changed. Can you thank him for it all? Is your answer "yes" or "not yet"? Explain your answer.

fifty pounds of carrots

We were in terrible financial straits. Terry had retired from the air force a few years before, and we'd settled in our new hometown in Wisconsin. There in the Wisconsin woods, Terry would find a wonderfully satisfying new career, and I would be a Writer, with a capital *W*. That was the dream, but we had some challenges on our way to fame and fortune. Jobs were hard to find. Writing didn't pay. Our savings account was soon exhausted. We had no money left in the checking account for food. Debt piled up as we waited for employment. We were Broke, with a capital *B*.

One morning—we had lots of time for Bible reading and prayer in those days—we read in 1 Kings 17:1–6 about how God had provided for Elijah in his time of need. "I have ordered the ravens to feed you," God said. That image stood out—ravens bringing Elijah food. Ravens as God's blessing delivery system. We wondered if God would send "ravens" to help us too. We prayed that he would.

And send them he did! Human ravens reached out to help us. Gifts of food, cash, and encouragement came our way. On the very day I talked to God about not having any grocery money, a friend gave us forty dollars. Balancing the family books on another day, I realized we were several hundred dollars short for the month. I talked to God about it. The very next day at church, a friend handed us an envelope. "I got a bonus at work. This is for you." Inside was a check in the amount of several hundred dollars. The exact amount I'd talked to God about.

There were other things too. When our daughter needed a winter jacket, a friend had one to hand down to her. A check from Grandma arrived on the very day the money was due for one of the children's school trips. We'd told no one about these specific needs—no one, that is, except God.

When a friend offered us a box of food from the Salvation Army food pantry, my first reaction wasn't gratitude. It was embarrassment. "But that food is for *poor* people," I protested. She looked at me with an unspoken "Well?" in her expression. I couldn't help but laugh. Of course we qualified! I accepted the box, humbled. Who was I to argue with God's raven?

The ravens came, but not because there is magic in prayer; there is no magic lamp to rub. God is not the genie in the bottle who appears to grant us our three wishes. He's not Santa, providing for good little boys and girls. We didn't repeat mantras or perform any rituals designed to inspire the heavenly powers to act on our behalf.

All we did was pray. We obeyed a divine command: "Cast all your anxiety on him because he cares for you" (1 Peter 5:7). We prayed. God heard. God cared. The ravens came in our time of need, not because of who we were or what we did, but because God is loving and kind, good and generous, able and willing to help in time of trouble.

"Jesus taught us to pray for our daily bread," writes Richard Foster in *Celebration of Discipline*. "Have you ever noticed that children ask for lunch in utter confidence that it will be provided? They have no need to stash away today's sandwiches for fear none will be available tomorrow. As far as they are concerned, there is an endless supply of sandwiches."

God has an endless supply ready for his children. One Saturday during those "raven days," I was making turkey soup (a huge pot with one big drumstick I'd bought on sale) and realized I had no carrots. Turkey water with an onion and some rice didn't sound too appetizing, but I couldn't justify using gas to make a special trip to town just for carrots. Besides, I'd already spent the grocery money for the week.

"Lord," I whined over the soup kettle, "I don't have any carrots."

The words were still hanging in the air in the kitchen when the phone rang. My friend Charlene was calling, asking, "Do you need any carrots?"

"What?" I asked, incredulous. She explained that her aunt rented some of her farmland to local Hmong farmers. They were done harvesting their beautiful gardens for the season. They'd left carrots in the field, and her aunt wondered if anyone wanted them.

Flabbergasted is how I felt. I grabbed some empty grocery bags, hopped in the car, and drove to the field. I knelt in the soft dirt at the beginning of one row of feathery green carrot tops. With my bare hands I reached forward, pushing my fingers through the silky soil. My fingers found carrots. I closed my hands around a bunch and lifted them from the earth. They were the most beautiful, perfect little carrots. I dropped them into the open bag at my side and dug again. And again. Soon I was harvesting carrots by the fistfuls.

I laughed and cried as I knelt there in that good earth, grateful to God, grateful to be gleaning what was left behind. Humbled under the eye of God, accepting his provision, on my knees. I filled one brown paper bag, then another, and a third. Why had I grabbed so many bags? Only God knew.

Back home, I couldn't resist weighing the bounty. Quantifying God's blessing is biblical. As the Israelites wandered the desert with Moses, God fed them with manna. (Check out Exodus 16.) How much manna? God provided an omer (evidently the recommended daily allowance for manna) per person per day. And God graciously provided two omers per person on the sixth day so they could take the Sabbath off. As the Israelites wandered, their clothing didn't wear out and (this is truly amazing) their feet didn't swell. For how long? Forty years. (I can't walk forty minutes without feeling a little tight in the tennies.) God provided for forty years! Another blessing quantified.

At the end of John's gospel, Jesus orchestrates a miraculous catch of fish for the disciples. How many fish did Jesus provide? Lots of fish. One hundred and fifty-three to be exact (John 21:11, in case you want to read it for yourself). When Jesus fed the crowd of five thousand men plus women and children, with only five loaves of bread and two fish, we're told the exact amount of the leftovers. Twelve basketfuls. (That proof is in Matthew 14:15–21.)

So I weighed the carrots. My rational mind needed to quantify God's provision. As if having *any* carrots wasn't miracle enough! But I went ahead and weighed God's goodness. How good was he? Over fifty pounds' of carrots worth.

Did I need carrots? Indeed.

Who knew my need? Only God.

Did God supply? Oh my, yes!

There's more. A couple of months later, on the Saturday morning before Thanksgiving, Terry and I sat in bed and discussed the sad state of our finances. We were both working by then, but we were still so far behind. Thanksgiving was coming. I reminded him that although the family was bringing parts of the meal to our house (relatives as ravens), and although we'd gotten a free turkey from my new employer (boss as another raven), there were still things we had to buy. And we didn't have much money left.

I asked him, "How can we afford to get everything we need—potatoes, onions, sweet potatoes, orange Jell-O, and all the rest—with just this little bit of cash?" We prayed.

Our "amen" was still hanging over the bed when the phone rang. It was Zelda, our elderly friend from church, and she sounded panicky. "Can you and Terry come over to my house right away?" Zelda needed us! We dressed in a rush and drove quickly to town. We walked into Zelda's kitchen. She smiled and pointed at a large cardboard box on her kitchen table.

"That's for you," she said. "I knew you wouldn't come if I told you why I wanted you to come over." The box was full of all the fixings for a traditional Thanksgiving meal. The box held all the things I had listed that morning—potatoes, onions, sweet potatoes, and more. Right down to the orange Jell-O.

God heard. God answered. In fact, he was answering that prayer before we'd even prayed it. Some people might call such things coincidence, but they don't know what I know. As Jesus explained it, "Your Father knows what you need before you ask him" (Matthew 6:8).

I know that an omniscient God watches over me, anticipating my needs, listening for my prayers, and timing his answers to bless me. I know that every time I need something—which is all the time—God is able *and willing* to provide.

And God has an endless supply. But to see that supply in personal terms? To apply that abundance to my daily need? This is the challenge, isn't it? To believe that God's endless supply is available to *us*. Available to me and to you. Now. Here. Today.

What is it you need today? Are you in need of a job, or a better one? Is it money you lack? Do you need a home? Do you need clothing or food? Do you need a friend? Do you need help? Answers? Comfort? Are you lonely? Are you afraid of the future? Afraid of changing? Are you angry? Are you tired? What is it you need today? Peace? Strength? Courage? Carrots?

God sent the ravens to provide what I needed. He did it not because I pray powerfully (I'm a wimp not a warrior, you'll recall). Not because I'm faithful. Not because I've earned his favor by being a good and dutiful daughter.

No, God provided simply because I am his child. I am his child and he loves me, and like all good fathers, God delights in blessing his children.

God "is able to do immeasurably more than all we ask or imagine, according to his power that is at work within us" (Ephesians 3:20). Ready to answer your prayers. Ready to supply your needs. Ready to work in your life.

Jesus said it in Matthew 7:7: "Ask and it will be given to you; seek and you will find; knock and the door will be opened to you." God is able, willing, and ready. When we called for help, he answered as if to say, "I thought you'd never ask!"

All you have to do is ask. Will you?

I sought the LORD, and he answered me;
he delivered me from all my fears.
—Psalm 34:4

points to ponder

1. What does it take to amaze you? (If you like to write, try freewriting for five or ten minutes beginning with "I'm amazed . . ." Set the timer. Keep your pen moving.)

2. Have you ever been needy? Describe the experience.

3. When have you experienced God's endless supply? What are you afraid to ask him for? Why are you hesitating?

the highway Bible

Picture it: Terry, me, three kids (one in an ankle cast), and two cats careening down the highway in a Ford Bronco, hauling an old Chevy hatchback on a two-wheeled trailer. Both vehicles are packed full of our stuff. We're on the road for the fourth day straight, driving from California to Minnesota.

It's late June—one of the hottest Junes on record, with temps above 100 degrees every day and a constant hot wind blasting. The boy's leg itches. The girls are antsy. The cats *m-r-r-owww!* their loud and constant complaint. We roast across the Mojave out of California and then chug up the steep grade to Flagstaff.

The route through Arizona and New Mexico and then north into Colorado is one long road-construction zone. Lanes merge and meander on and off narrow shoulders, with orange plastic barrels the only division between vehicles passing each other—barely—at breakneck speeds. Yikes!

Each time we enter one of these narrow places, the truck sways, buffeted by the wind and pulled off center by the weight of the fishtailing trailer. Terry navigates—barely!—between concrete barriers. I shut my eyes, white-knuckle the edge of the front seat, and holler, "Hang on, kids!"

My reaction becomes a little joke among them. At one motel restaurant, I bump the table as we sit down. Terry grabs the table's edge as he sways back and forth yelling, "Hang on, kids!" They all join in, laughing. Very funny. Can I help it if I believe expecting the worst means you'll never be disappointed?

On our fifth morning, we head east out over the Colorado flats toward Nebraska. About an hour into that morning's travel, I glance back and notice the Chevy's hatchback lid bouncing open. How long it had been open, I didn't know.

"Stop!" I shout. Terry maneuvers to the side of the road. We get out of the truck and walk to the back of the Chevy. Everything seems to be in place in the trunk. Perhaps we haven't lost anything. We slam the trunk shut and continue on our way.

That night at the next motel, I search for but can't find my Bible. My new Bible, the one I'd purchased just a few years before, when I returned to church, returned to God. My precious Bible—God's Word!—that had brought me solace and comfort. I'd written personal notes and marked significant passages in that Bible. I'd poured out my heart to God over those pages, cried onto them, prayed over them. That Bible held a record of my hopes and my sorrows. It was a memorial to my dreams. A remembrance of my journey.

My Bible that I'd packed that morning in the back of the Chevy. My Bible that had evidently bounced out onto the highway, somewhere in the western wilderness.

Oh, the sad thought of my poor Bible lying in a ditch, pounded by rain, sleet, wind, and hail. The thought of it crushed into the asphalt by an eighteen-wheeler. The thought of my poor Bible—more friend than book—in a muddy, horrible mess on a lonely highway was too much to bear. Too much!

In the middle of mourning my loss, I saw *him*. In my mind's eye, a shadow first, then the form of a man, a hitchhiker, walking along that stretch of Colorado highway. I saw him stop to rest at the roadside, saw him glance down, and then saw him pick up the tattered book lying there. He opened it then, to the exact verse, the precise passage of Scripture, that God had ordained for him to read there.

I imagined a glimmer of sun, of knowing, filtering down on the weary traveler. A ray of hope warming him there as he read my Bible, his mind changing, his life altering, his eyes opening to see truth, light, and love. I saw him tucking my Bible—his Bible—into his backpack and standing up taller and smiling. Smiling and walking on toward home.

God says that his Word "will not return to me empty, but will accomplish what I desire and achieve the purpose for which I sent it" (Isaiah 55:11). A Bible in the motel-room drawer offers comfort to one traveler, conviction to another. A Bible on a highway, lost to the original owner, might offer an encouraging word just in time to another.

I walked into a hotel room once, and there on the bed was the Gideon Bible lying open. I know God's hand when I see it. I read the open pages and found perfect advice for me that day. But what blessed me most was the thought that someone on the cleaning crew had cared enough to leave the open Bible there. They wanted to welcome the next visitor to this place, perhaps had prayed for the traveler (me!) who would be staying in that room, in that city, on that night. Thank you, whoever you are, for such a blessing!

My aunt worked as a housekeeper for the Radisson Hotel in downtown Minneapolis years ago. She stole a Bible. (Does stealing a Bible carry a sentence to hell, without possibility of parole?) "Placed by the Gideons" is embossed in gold on the Bible's cover. I know this because I'm looking at it right now. The Bible my aunt stole ended up at our house, in my room, in my hands. Its pages are yellowed and flaking, and the binding is dried and cracking. I wrote my name and address inside the front cover in childish, grade-school scrawl. I claimed the book as my own.

It was my first Bible, the only Bible in our house. And it was mine. It was placed by the Gideons—God bless them!—into my hands, placed by God into my heart. I underlined one verse: John 3:16. It's all I needed to know. All I'll ever need to know.

Today I have a bunch of Bibles, and Bible software on my computer, giving me instant access to several translations and commentaries at a keystroke. What good are my Bibles if they sit on the shelf? What good is the software if I don't access the program? Is the Bible a museum piece, like a trophy on a hunter's wall—lifeless proof of my skill as a buyer?

My mother, a lifelong agnostic, became a de facto Bible collector in her later years. She had several Bibles on the shelf in her apartment, each a gift from one or another of her children, each child trying, with another translation, to open her eyes and heart to God.

"Let's try a modern translation that might be easier for her to understand. Let's try a large-print Bible this time. Her eyes are going." After properly thanking the giver, she'd place each Bible in turn on the shelf. What good did they do there?

God's Word is alive. Not just symbols on paper, but a voice, calling from the shelf, "Come away for a while and read. Life's starved hearts, come feast on real food, lasting substance." God's Word is alive, and he accomplishes his purposes through it.

My mother's Bibles sat on the shelf, but even as they sat there, they bore silent witness. The voice called, patiently, relentlessly. Eventually she listened. My mother dusted off her shelf, dusted off her heart, and believed. She was eighty-five years old.

God's Word is alive. I prayed one day that God's Word would be alive in someone else's life, praying for that person that Hebrews 4:12 would be true for them: "For the word of God is living and active. Sharper than any double-edged sword, it penetrates even to dividing soul and spirit, joints and marrow; it judges the thoughts and attitudes of the heart."

I stopped in the middle of the prayer. *How dare I pray this for someone else and not for myself? How dare I pray to invoke this kind of power in another person's life and not be willing to have this power working in my life?* I changed my prayer. "Lord, change *me*. Make your Word come alive for me. Let it be sharp, a sword penetrating *my* heart. Let it judge *my* thoughts and *my* attitudes. Teach *me* your ways, Lord." God's Word is alive.

The Bible I read most often these days is the Bible Terry bought me to replace what has become known as "the Highway Bible." He inscribed the replacement, "A new Bible for our new life."

It's full of notes, arrows, and smiling faces—blobs and splashes. I've underlined or circled words or phrases that touched me on a particular day. On page 1517 are these words from Jesus: "'Have faith in God. . . . I tell you, whatever you ask for in prayer, believe that you have received it, and it will be yours'" (Mark 11:22, 24). It's his way of saying, "Hang on, kids!"

Next to these verses, I jotted a date—over a decade ago now—and the words "God has been faithful!" I wrote that note during a time of struggle. I've added to that note again and again.

Four years later, in other trials, I wrote, "Wow! Has he been faithful!" Two years after that I added, "Yes, God! You are faithful!" drawing a heart that time. A year later I added, "Amen! *Still* faithful!" and two years later, "Oh *yes!* Lord, you are faithful indeed!"

It's a confession of my faith, a reminder for me, a reassurance of what I know is true. That God has been faithful through troubled times when hot, dry winds buffeted us. God has been faithful when we careened through narrow paths and took scary curves too fast. God has been faithful through serious health issues and family struggles, as we itched, sweated, and squirmed, whining and wailing our complaints. God has been faithful. He's helped us to hang on.

And today, in the middle of today's troubles, heading toward tomorrow's troubles, I will say it again. God is faithful indeed!

My "new" Bible is smudged, blobbed, marked, splashed, creased, and tear-stained. My Bible—God's word for *me*—is worn, dirty, and wonderful.

Do you have a Bible? God, the author, invites you to open the pages and come along for the ride of your life. Read it. Write in it. Underline, comment, wonder, question, and exclaim all over its pages. *Yes, God! Faithful indeed! Thank you, Lord!* Open the pages and hang on! Make it *your* Bible—God's alive, sharp, powerful, penetrating word for you.

Let it be God's word *for you*. Let it be *your* Bible—worn, dirty, and altogether wonderful.

The grass withers and the flowers fall,
but the word of the Lord stands forever.
—1 Peter 1:24–25

points to ponder

1. What is your most prized possession? What makes it so special? Have you ever lost something precious? Tell the story (in writing, if you'd like.) How did you handle the loss?

2. To write in your Bible or not to write in your Bible? That is the question. Which side are you on? Defend your position. Now defend the opposite view.

3. If you don't have a Bible, why not get one this week? Ask a friend or the staff at your local religious bookstore for advice if you're wondering about the different Bibles available. God has so much to say to you in his Word. Start reading it for yourself. If you already have your own Bible, consider buying one for a friend or donating one to a local prison ministry or women's shelter. Share God's Word.

worrywart

Is it just me, or are all mothers hardwired to worry? My children are adults and don't need daily parental care anymore. They're mostly out of the house, but I still worry about them.

Three of our daughters are married and running their own households. One of them even has her own index-card file system, another has a chore chart in her home, and the third uses a computerized menu-planning program. Two of our sons-in-law love to cook, and one of our boys is even a chef. I know they can feed themselves, but I still worry.

Since I'm no longer doling out the Flintstones vitamins, how can I be sure they are getting enough A, B, C, and D? Are they eating well-balanced meals, or are they—free at last—pigging out on Pop-Tarts and Cheetos? (Oh, to be a mouse in their houses.)

They can find their own clothing. Yet I worry that, just starting out in their careers, they might not be "dressing for success." So I try to help by buying them gifts of clothing for birthdays and holidays. You'd think I'd know better, after all the time I've spent on the front lines of the Mall Wars.

The wars began when one daughter hit middle school and begged for a shirt so small I thought it was a tube sock. I fired the first round of refusals, continuing to fight the pants that showed more fanny than fabric and the heels so high—for a middle school dance, no less—that it wasn't safe to walk in them without a net. I fought valiantly against the boys' sloppy shirts and baggy pants, body jewelry, and purple hair. I refused to fork over the cash for the latest fads—shoes costing more than the house payment, for instance.

It should come as no surprise to me, then, that, free at last, they are not listening to my fashion advice. But I just don't understand why my grown-up son exchanged the light blue oxford shirt I bought him for something baggy in a wild print. I don't get it, especially when his dad looks so handsome in those button-down collars.

The kids may have "come a long way, baby," but I haven't. It was a short step for me from "Look both ways before you cross the street and don't talk to strangers" to "Be careful driving to that job interview and watch out for weirdos!" And it wasn't much of a leap from "Don't forget your mittens or your hands will freeze off" to "Don't forget your gloves or your fingers will freeze off."

If I stop worrying, who will be awake in the middle of the night waiting for the call from the police, letting us know that the kids *did* end up "in a ditch somewhere" just like I warned them would happen if they insisted on taking those country curves so fast. (So it hasn't happened in thirty years. Why stop worrying now?)

God gave me a big job to do: Keep them clean. ("Don't sleep with bubble gum or you'll be sorry. Especially if we're out of peanut butter!") Teach them to clean themselves. ("Yes, you must wash *both* hands before supper, and not just the hand you use to push the food onto your fork!")

Kiss their boo-boos. ("Yes, honey, it was mean of the side-walk man to put that big bump right there in front of your roller skate!") Mend their torn jeans. ("You climbed where? To get *what*?")

Check their homework. ("This is math? When did they change it?") Civilize them. ("Next time, *don't* tell Aunt Frieda that she smells funny. Just say ... well, just don't say anything!")

Dole out the Flintstones. ("Pebbles for you ... and Bam-Bam for you ... Stop crying! You had Pebbles yesterday. And no, you can't have dibs on every Dino!") Tuck them in at night. ("Yes, you should 'God bless' Aunt Frieda, even if she does smell funny.")

It's been a big job. It's been a lot of worry. How can a mother not worry?

"Let go and let God," I've heard. Oh, I've prayed plenty in the last thirty years. Back when the kids were in diapers. (*Lord, which end of this diaper is up? Which end of this kid is up?*) Back when they were in grade school. (*Lord, keep this tired old car running ... and this tired old mom too?*) Back when they were teenagers. (*Lord, how come there isn't a cure for stupidity? Please put some extra angels on guard.*)

I've prayed, yes, but letting go is another story altogether. "Release everything to God. Give him your cares and troubles." Easier said than done. But easier to do, I'm learning, when I understand the reality of my relationship with God.

We are branches, the Bible says, and God is the vine. I don't live in wine country, so vines and branches are confusing to me. The image of a tree and branches works better for forest dwellers like me. God is the tree and I am a branch. I get it. I understand that analogy. As a branch, I have no responsibility for my care and upkeep. I'm just simply attached to the tree.

This is the picture of complete dependence. The branches don't have any responsibility. The tree does everything. Does the branch decide daily, "I think I'll be attached to the tree today"? No. The branch is simply attached. What must the branch do? Receive. Simply receive.

I am dependent on God, like a branch depends on the tree. Does that mean I have *no* responsibility for doing, being, saying, thinking, or acting on anything? Of course not. I *do* have responsibility, but only the responsibility that *God* assigns me. And at this stage in my life, praying for my children is my assigned responsibility.

That sounds great. How does it work in real life? How does it relate to "letting go and letting God"? How does it affect a worrywart? Too often I forget that I'm only the branch and that he is the tree. Too often I take on responsibility for something when that responsibility belongs to God. And that leads to worrying. Worrying isn't my job. Praying is.

As the children were growing up, I had tasks to perform, and I was accountable to God for doing them to the best of my ability, according to the gifts he gave me. But the *responsibility* for my children's lives was never mine. The responsibility for life belongs to the one on whom we depend for life, the one who gives us the gift of life: God himself.

As their mother, praying for the children has always been my number one job. I'm the only one who could pray a mother's prayers for them. Think about it. If you don't pray for your children, who will? Others might pray, but no one else will pray with the concern and dedication of a mother.

My children in turn have a need—a responsibility—to recognize that they are absolutely dependent on God. I can't do that for them. It's not my job. It's my job to pray for them, to pray that they will realize their dependence and draw near to God.

We are all dependent on God, whether we like to admit it or not. Think about it. If God didn't permit it, we wouldn't make it across the street. We can't get out of bed but for the grace of God. We don't *make* ourselves utterly dependent on him; we *are* utterly dependent on him. It's not about putting ourselves in a dependent position; it's about *recognizing* our dependent condition.

I draw my next breath only by the grace of God. Doesn't that put it all in perspective? God is in control. We don't put him in charge; he *is* in charge. We have but to acknowledge that fact in our lives. "He is before all things, and in him all things hold together" (Colossians 1:17). Once we recognize God's sovereignty over us, we are on the right road. Releasing all to God then becomes a logical act. He has it all anyway. Why carry burdens we don't need to bear?

Let go and let God. How do we do that? There are three ways to let go:

1. Pray.
2. Pray.
3. Pray.

There is no other way to release your concerns to God than to pray. No self-help mantra or positive affirmation will do it. No magic formula or glitzy gimmick will bring you peace. You won't find what you're looking for in any book or article promising you ten ways or thirty days to a better life. Only prayer will give you what you need.

You won't find what you need within yourself; you are a cul-de-sac. Around and around you'll go, but you'll make no progress. You need the wide-open, infinite superhighway of help. You need God. Only in prayer will you find the peace you seek.

Only in prayer.

Prayer is good for worrywarts like me. "Do not be anxious about anything, but in everything, by prayer and petition, with thanksgiving, present your requests to God" (Philippians 4:6). Worrying, it seems, is not an option. Prayer and trust are worry's antidotes, and peace is God's promise.

God can handle what concerns me and my children. God has the hairs on their heads numbered—something I never found time for (though as the boys get older, that might become less time-consuming). God has the number of their days already calculated—something I don't *want* to know!

God is the one who knows their thoughts, their needs, their dreams, and their futures. I am just their mother, and as much as the eyes in the back of my head, my intuition, and my snooping have helped, I admit I still don't know *everything*.

It makes sense to release my worries to God.

Lord, I'm worried about the kids. Today I take the three-by-five prayer cards I have for each of my children. (I have my organized moments. Who knows how long this one will last.) I kneel in a sunny spot on the living-room carpet and lay the cards before me on the floor.

Lord, today I release these children to you. These are your children, not mine. They've lived in my home, eaten at my table, slept under my roof, but they are now, as they've always been, yours. I had the privilege of raising them, of watching them grow and learn, but they've always belonged to the future, always been part of a separate plan you had in mind for them before they were even conceived.

I release my children to you, Lord, trusting you for their days to come. Thank you for the job—and the joy—of being their mother.

Praying brings peace, but I'm still tempted to worry. And not just about my own children. The cardinals built a nest this spring in the evergreen bush outside my home-office window. I worried as I watched the young parents-to-be build the nest. Was this the best location to raise a family—so low to the ground, with neighborhood cats on the prowl? I worried during the incubation period as wind and rain blasted the bush. I worried when I saw the new hatchlings, and I warned the pest control guy not to spray too close to the nursery.

Then the other day I noticed a young cardinal—transformed in just days, it seemed, from a scrawny sack of fragile bones to a boisterous, demanding adolescent—flapping its wings at the nest's edge.

"Get back in that nest!" I hollered through the glass. "You're too little to be out there on your own!" With teenage bravado, he flap-hopped to the nearest branch.

Both his parents squawked at him. I didn't need to speak Cardinal to know what they were saying. "Look both ways before you cross the fields. Don't talk to cats. And take shelter when the snow flies or your wings will freeze off!"

I added, "And call your mother once in a while. She'll be worrying!"

Do not be anxious about anything, but in everything, by prayer and petition, with thanksgiving, present your requests to God. And the peace of God, which transcends all understanding, will guard your hearts and your minds in Christ Jesus.

—Philippians 4:6–7

points to ponder

1. What does it mean to be independent? How independent are you? What does it mean to be dependent? On what or on whom are you dependent?

2. Make a list of your responsibilities. Which are truly yours? Which will you release to God today?

3. Imagine you have a bunch of helium balloons. Imagine writing your worries, troubles, and heartaches on them and releasing them, one by one, to God. (Don't try to pull them back! Let them go.) Write about the experience of letting them go. (For full effect, try this with real balloons.)

petty peeves

We used to have a local TV meteorologist—I'll call him Chuck—who drove me crazy. (He's since moved on to some other market. I kind of miss the aggravation.) Chuck could not make up his mind. "Looks like a stormy day," he'd say and then instantly modify his forecast. "Well, it won't really be stormy, but it is going to rain. Hard."

Okay, I'd think, *we could use a good hard rain*, but then Chuck changed his mind. "Well, it probably won't rain *too* hard, but it *is* going to be a wet one out there. You may want to bring your umbrella." *At last, some useful information*, I'd think, until Chuck clarified once more. "Well, only if you're going to go outside."

Thanks, Chuck. All this time I've been using my umbrella inside the house! Duh! I feel like an idiot. Well, not really an idiot, just not very smart.

"Later, possibly even later . . ." Chuck said once, and I wondered, *What time would that be?* Chuck explained, ". . . as early as late tonight . . ." *"As early as late"? Huh? How early is late, Chuck? Nine? Ten? Midnight? Two a.m.?*

Continuing, Chuck predicted, ". . . we'll have storms on and off. It's going to be partly cloudy." I hadn't known that early was late, and I'd never realized the definition of "partly cloudy" was "storms on and off," but then I'm not a trained meteorologist like Chuck.

One day Chuck seemed especially worked up. "There's a whopper of a storm heading our way," he began, his voice agitated. My heart beat a little faster. Thunderstorms are exciting. I pictured myself waiting out the storm, hunkered down in the basement with my flashlight, a battery-operated radio, my favorite blanket, and a bag of tortilla chips. In the few seconds it took to decide whether to take the cheese dip or the salsa with me, Chuck modified his forecast. "Well, it's not really a whopper of a storm, but a big storm . . ." *Okay, a big storm. That's still worth getting excited about.*

Chuck continued, "Well, not such a big storm, but high winds are coming." *High winds, Chuck? How high?*

As if he read my mind, Chuck said, "Well, not *high* winds, not like a *tornado*, but it *is* going to be gusty out there."

Gusty, Chuck? Big deal! I was looking forward to braving fierce weather, but for "gusty," I didn't need the basement. I did need the tortilla chips, however, and was crunching the first one down when Chuck summed it up, true to form: "Actually, nothing severe until tomorrow, and that's not going to be severe."

It bugged me that Chuck was always hedging. He hedged because he knew that people would blame him for the weather, for ruining their plans, or for making them worry about something that never materialized. He hedged because he didn't want anyone beating him up while he was in line at McDonald's. ("I'd like a Big Mac and a large fry. Well, not just one large fry, but an order of fries. No, wait. Make that a small fry and some Chicken McNuggets. No, wait . . .")

Hedging was Chuck's insurance. Nobody can blame a weatherman for weather he didn't actually predict. Chuck avoided predicting weather as often as he could. That's probably why Chuck got so wound up whenever severe weather did come our way. He couldn't avoid it.

In the middle of a raging thunderstorm, Chuck broke into our regularly scheduled programming to bring us a severe weather update. On camera in his shirtsleeves—live from the TV station's weather center instead of the usual news set—Chuck filled us in on the latest breaking weather news. He spoke at three times his normal rate, his voice an octave higher than usual.

"There's pea-to-marble-sized hail falling right now," he squeaked. He said it so fast that "pea-to-marble" sounded like "pita marble." Just how big is a pita marble? I'll bet Chuck didn't even know.

Revved up now, Chuck rattled on breathlessly, tossing around terms like "tornadic" and "upper-level disturbance" with abandon. In moments like these, Chuck felt no need to hedge. He couldn't be wrong. The weather he was predicting was already occurring. Chuck was off the hook.

"Chuckisms" are part of our life now. We even make up our own, just to bug each other.

"This butter is really hard," Terry said at breakfast the other day. "Well, not really hard. Just not really soft."

"And this coffee tastes disgusting," I said, adding, "Well, not really disgusting, just terrible. Well, not terrible. Just not real good."

"It's going to be a crazy day at the office," Terry predicted and then hedged with, "Well, not really crazy, just a little hectic. What's the weather supposed to be?"

"Chuck said we're going to have 'significant rainfall,' but then he said a few, light scattered showers."

"Uh-oh," Terry said. "We're in for a downpour then. Well, maybe not a downpour, but I'd better take my umbrella, huh?"

"Only if you're going outside."

"Brilliant," Terry said.

"I learned that from Chuck," I said. (Good luck, Chuck, in your new job, and thanks for the material.)

Okay, I admit it. I am a petty, petty person. Chuck really bugged me. Other things bug me too. The former news anchor on Chuck's station had weird eyebrows. It peeved me the way they formed a triangle in the middle of his forehead when the studio lights hit him a certain way. I never heard a word of the news, so intent was I on watching that triangle appear and disappear.

I'm a petty, peevish person. The list of my pet peeves goes on and on. I live a small, self-absorbed, bugged, pettily peevish life. I am puny. God is large. That's why I got a little nervous reading Andrew Murray's prayer in *Absolute Surrender*. Murray writes, "Let my life be a proof of what an omnipotent God can do." Do I dare pray this? Do I dare pray an omnipotent, all-powerful God into my petty, puny, peevish life?

God is huge. I live small. My petty, puny little life doesn't have the capacity to contain God in all his power and might. I was afraid I'd explode if I prayed God's omnipotence into my life, but I decided to try it anyway. I had nothing to lose. I couldn't get any pettier.

When we pray, "Let my life be a proof of what an omnipotent God can do," our lives begin to be a proof, not of who *we* are or what *we* can do, but a proof of what *God* can do.

God can take the petty and the puny, the weak and the wimpy, the half-baked and the completely fried, and he can do something wonderful. How? Not because we have anything to offer, but because God is able to do so much with so little.

Do we really bring *nothing* to the equation? What about our talents and abilities? Certainly God has given gifts to each one of us. But what we have is nothing compared to the omnipotence and power of God! I get into trouble when I start to think that I have something God needs. Help from my inner giant maybe? My vast compassion? My amazing patience? Ha!

I get into trouble when I start thinking that my abilities, if I have any at all, are a happy accident, that I got lucky at birth. I forget that all I have, all I am, comes from him. I forget that "every good and perfect gift is from above, coming down from the Father of the heavenly lights, who does not change like shifting shadows" (James 1:17).

I get into trouble when I forget the Giver and start celebrating the gifts.

I have nothing to bring to my relationship with God but need. Deep helplessness is what I have, all I have to offer an omnipotent God. Of course, if I choose to believe God is less than omnipotent, less than all-powerful, then that's another story. Then I can design any kind of god I want.

He can be a genie at my beck and call, or Santa Claus, or the wind, or a rock. But then I'm in charge, not God, and I know where that's led me in the past. Into petty self-absorption. Into limited living. Right back where I started.

I want more. I want to see God for who he really is—all-powerful, all-knowing, and always present. Omnipotent, omniscient, and omnipresent. The omni God. My only response to the presence of *this* God in my life will be, as Murray described it, "deep helplessness and simple childlike rest." Simply trusting.

"Let my life be a proof of what an omnipotent God can do." What will be the evidence of an omnipotent God's power and presence in my life? I can think of some possible ways my life might be different.

If I realize that the omnipotent God is at work in my life, I might worry less about money and argue less with Terry about spending and bills. I'll pray, specifically identifying my worries, and ask God to guide my decisions.

Let's say I'm worried about my career, worried that I'll run out of ideas. With such petty fear driving me, every time I go to the bookstore I'll be consumed with insecurity and envy, thinking, *I should have written that. All the good ideas are already taken.* I'll worry that my writing stinks, become paralyzed by these worries, call it "writer's block," and spend my days examining the TV news anchor's eyebrows and criticizing the weatherman's style.

On the other hand, if I recognize that God is omnipotent and at work in my career, I might pray, specifically identifying my worries and releasing them to him. Spend time exploring God's Word. Realize that he is the Author of everything and has an infinite supply of good ideas.

I will bear no responsibility beyond putting my rear end into my chair each day and remaining open to his leading. Having done my work, I'll learn to trust him for the results. I will resolve in my mind, once and for all, that God—*omni* God—will provide what I need day by day. (I'm excited just thinking about it!)

"Lord, make my life a proof of what you, the omnipotent God, can do." I pray that prayer and imagine a new life. I see myself less petty and more relaxed. I see a new me, settled and content, centered on the truth of God's Word. I sense a new confidence, a new trust, that this omnipotent God will accomplish every one of his purposes in my life, in his time.

"Let my life be a proof of what an omnipotent God can do," Murray prayed. Do I have the courage to pray it? Do I have the courage to grab on to the back end of a roaring train and let it take me where it will? Do I have the guts to pray this and then just hold on and let God take me wherever he pleases?

Do I dare to pray it? Do you?

Whatever is true, whatever is noble, whatever is right, whatever is pure, whatever is lovely, whatever is admirable—if anything is excellent or praiseworthy—think about such things.

—Philippians 4:8

points to ponder

1. What is the number one pet peeve on your list? Why does it bug you so much? What, if anything, can you do about it?

2. How is the life of a person who trusts in God different from the life of a person who trusts in self? Give specific examples.

3. Do you believe that God is omnipotent, omniscient, and omnipresent? What evidence have you found that he is or is not?

the cuisinart of prayer

Bless the prayer warrior who is on her knees before dawn, praying those eloquent prayers that inspire prodigals homeward and change the course of human events. May the Lord give her strength! I confess I've never been much of an "on my knees" kind of pray-er, but I've prayed in almost every other possible position.

I've prayed standing at the kitchen sink, up to my elbows in dirty dishwater. *Lord, why isn't anyone helping me? Why do I have to do all the work around here?* Okay, those prayers qualify more as whining than praying and sound vaguely familiar. I hear myself as a young girl. "Mommy, how come my brother doesn't have to help me with the dishes?" I've been practicing that kind of praying all my life.

I've prayed bent in half with my head in the oven in a holiday panic. (Not to worry. The oven is electric, not gas.) *Please, Lord, don't let anyone notice the black scorch marks on the backside of this turkey. May the rest of the Thanksgiving meal make up for this bird's sorry state.* The guests, thankfully, didn't notice the bird's problem, but they commented on the stuffing's crunchy mystery bits. They pondered the possibilities all through dinner. "What are they? Walnuts? Pecans? Bread crusts?" I prayed silently, *Oh Lord, please don't let them be the end of the rubber scraper.* I hadn't noticed the end of the scraper was missing until after I'd stuffed the bird. The Cuisinart might have eaten it (it might be possessed) while I chopped the celery for the stuffing. I can't be sure, so I refuse to be held responsible.

I prayed the next day seated on our old couch. I intended, when I sat down, to pray for the whole world but then narrowed my focus to my organizational challenges, like keeping better track of kitchen utensils. Rubber scrapers, for instance. At that moment, the couch's broken spring poked me in the thigh—a pointed reminder of another need. *Lord, please help me find the meat thermometer.* If I'd had it the day before, I wouldn't have been serving blackened turkey.

I've prayed sitting on the piano bench in church on Sunday mornings because I don't really play the piano. I'm mostly self-taught and certainly not polished, and I have never—*never*—enjoyed playing in front of people (except my dad, of course). But our little church needed a pianist and nobody else seemed to be volunteering, so I did. I guess I was the answer to other people's prayers, though that's hard for me to imagine.

One memorable Sunday I sat there, praying for my nervous stomach, my trembling knees, and my shaking hands. And elbows. The organist nodded in my direction from the other side of the pulpit. It was time to start our duet. In a flash (amazing how fast the mind works under stress), I pictured my son at his first piano recital when he was six. I'd forced lessons on him since I'd never had many myself. I was certain he was a prodigy, certain, that is, until that recital.

He gave it his all, pouring himself into the song, completely unaware—though the audience quickly became painfully aware—that while his left hand played a deft accompaniment, his right hand was positioned one key off the melody. What a difference one little key makes!

So there I sat, in that moment between the organist's first measure and my cue to join her on the second measure as we'd discussed, my mind somewhere in the past. *Lord, help,* I prayed as I played my first measure. The organist looked up at me, surprised. I listened to what she was playing and wondered, *What is she playing? She's messing everything up!*

A sarcastic little voice answered the question. *She's playing the* first *song of the morning* first. *What a novel approach!* With horror, I realized I'd started with our second selection. The sarcastic voice had a suggestion. *Perhaps you'd like to get on the same page?* I flipped quickly to the correct song, the song I'd marked with a big yellow sticky note on which I'd written a big "#1." In red. So I wouldn't miss it.

As I played, I sensed prayers from the congregation. Prayers for me, I thought, or maybe prayers for my replacement. It was hard to be sure. Until my replacement showed up a month later, my own prayers on that piano bench were for nimble fingers and a tone-deaf audience. God provided both, on alternating Sundays.

I've done a lot of praying sitting behind the wheel of various vehicles. (Did I mention I failed my driver's test? Twice? I just didn't get the whole parallel-parking thing. Did you know that running over one of those orange cones counts as an accident and is cause for automatic failure?) I've prayed in parking lots (see above), and I've prayed at stoplights for the police to catch that driver who just raced through as it turned red. For the police not to notice when I do that. (Did you know that's against the law?)

I've prayed in the car in the dark as I've inched down a snow-covered highway in the middle of a January night, following a snowplow. Could the fact that the snowplow was there clearing the way have been the answer? (Duh!) I've prayed as the car slid off a country road in the middle of the worst blizzard in a decade and settled nose first into a snowbank. A helpful farmer materialized out of nowhere a few minutes later, in his truck with a tow chain. He looked a lot like an angel to me.

I prayed one night as I drove home in our Bronco in freezing rain. I prayed as I headed up the steep hill on our country road, four-wheel drive engaged. A simple prayer: "Please? Please? Please?" The truck moved forward more and more slowly. I prayed as the forward motion stopped on the ice beneath the tires, another simple prayer: "Oh-oh, oh-oh!" The truck paused midhill, then started sliding backward, slowly at first, then faster and faster as I prayed an increasingly frantic, "Oh no, *oh no*!" That became a combination prayer of "Oh, oh, *please no!*" changing to a plaintive "Help! Help!" as I tried to steer backward through the dark to avoid the neighbors' mailbox.

I prayed, "Stop me! Stop me!" as I neared the four-foot-deep drainage ditch next to their driveway. The truck stopped sliding inches from the edge. I'd already imagined the truck perpendicular to the earth, its tailgate in the ditch. I'd pictured myself sitting in the driver's seat staring up at the black-as-pitch night sky, the cold sleet pelting the windshield. Then, the truck safely horizontal and standing still, I prayed—more of an exhale of relief actually—"Thank you, thank you, thank you, Lord!"

I've prayed in other positions in other places too. I've prayed at the bus stop for the bus to come on time as I waited in a thunderstorm. I've prayed for safe arrivals and departures while I waited at airports. I've prayed in bed while staring at the ceiling, waiting for my back to heal, waiting for labor to end, waiting for the flu to pass. I've prayed walking the halls of hospitals and standing at hospital bedsides, waiting for others to heal.

I've prayed at the kitchen table while helping my daughter with her math homework. *Please help her understand fractions. But first help me remember how they work.* I thanked God for the miracle when she raised her D average to a C–. I've prayed at the mall and in stores while shopping—praying for bargains and self-control and finding both. More miracles!

But I've never been an "on my knees" kind of pray-er. I don't know how the monks do it kneeling on cold, hard monastery floors. I'm not a religious sister kneeling at the rail of a grand cathedral. I'm not one of the sainted church fathers (or mothers) kneeling in the dirt or on the hard wooden floor of a simple chapel. I'm none of those.

I'm a "pray on the run, pray as you go" kind of pray-er. And I've wondered if that's okay with God. Do those kinds of prayers count? Are those prayers worth praying? *Are they worth listening to, Lord?*

Yes. Yes. Yes. "Pray without ceasing," the Bible says (1 Thessalonians 5:17 KJV). How can we possibly, practically, pray without ceasing unless we learn to pray on the fly? A sincere prayer offered from any position at any time, an honest crying out to God from the depths of the heart, from the heart of my need, will always be heard.

I know that's true. Yet I've wondered if there is something more. Is there something special about "on the knees" praying? Something I was missing?

One Tuesday afternoon, I stood at the stove, stirring spaghetti sauce for supper. As I stirred, I read the prologue of Charles Colson's book *Loving God*. Colson, a successful lawyer and presidential advisor, landed in prison for his part in the Watergate scandal of the 1970s. After his release from prison, he founded the Prison Fellowship ministry.

Colson said his life before prison had been "the perfect success story, the great American dream fulfilled." But the awards and accolades, the prestige and position, the trappings of his success, were not what God used in starting the ministry to the imprisoned. "All my achievements meant nothing in God's economy," Colson wrote.

I imagined this man, so proud, so powerful, and so self-sufficient, and then I pictured him in prison, his power, position, and pride stripped away. I saw him broken and sorry. I imagined how he might have prayed then, on his knees on the cold concrete of the cell floor, broken not just before the world but before God. I imagined him there on his knees, humbled under God's mighty hand.

Was that what it took to bring him to his knees? What, I wondered, would it take for me?

Colson continued: "The real legacy of my life was my biggest failure—that I was an ex-convict. My greatest humiliation—being sent to prison—was the beginning of God's greatest use of my life; He chose the one experience in which I could not glory for *His* glory."

So God could use our biggest failures for his glory. I thought about how God had taken the broken pieces of my life—my sins and my sorrows, my wimpiness and my worries—and was using them for a purpose. My fumblings and failures were becoming the bedrock of whatever opportunity I had to touch other people, whether through writing and speaking or in my personal relationships. Those terrible things were the very things God could use to bring healing and hope to others.

I saw it then, the truth that almighty God cared enough to listen when I prayed. Cared enough to make his power, that power that is able to bring life from death—resurrection power—available when I prayed. Resurrection power is what I was tapping into when I prayed—every time, everywhere, in whatever position, I prayed. A new sense of the willingness of almighty God to enter into my experience, into my life, and into my heart hit me. And humbled me. Humbled by the wonder of it all, I fell to my knees, right there in front of the stove, and prayed.

> Praise be to . . . the God of all comfort, who comforts us in all our troubles, so that we can comfort those in any trouble with the comfort we ourselves have received from God.
> —2 Corinthians 1:3–4

points to ponder

1. Describe a moment when you experienced a feeling of sheer panic. How did you cope? Describe a moment of complete peace. Where did it come from?

2. "Pray without ceasing," the Bible says. Is it possible? Why or why not?

3. When has God brought good out of a bad experience for you? Who has comforted you in times of trouble? What situation needs God's touch today?

kitchen cathedral

It was a gray October morning. The temperature was nippy—nippier than it should have been at that time of year. Chuck the weatherman explained on the morning news that a cold air mass pressing down from Canada was to blame. "It's an arctic air mass," Chuck said. "Well, not really *arctic*, but very cold."

We'd even had snow the day before. "It's too early for snow," Chuck said. "Well, not really too early, I guess, because we have it." Another brilliant observation. (I miss Chuck. Really I do.)

Terry bundled up that morning as he left for work. As he put on his gloves and wrapped his scarf around his neck, he said, "Too early for gloves and a scarf. Well, not really, I guess, since I'm wearing them." We both laughed.

As Terry went out the back door, Izzy, the Fox Terrorist, trotted to the living room to assume her position on the top of the couch, where she keeps her vigil over the back deck. (Woe to the varmints whose hapless wanderings take them into the Terrorist's line of sight.) Izzy perches on top of the couch so often that both of the couch's back cushions have permanent dents the size of her body. Terry told the last person who asked about the dents, "It's not a couch; it's a very expensive dog bed."

I knew Izzy was getting comfortable in the living room, but I didn't want that to happen. I wanted some quiet time and knew I couldn't have it if she was free to start whining and barking at the squirrels. (Just a whisper of the word *squirrel* sends her into a tailspin. We have to spell s-q-u-i-r-r-e-l in front of her. Even now, I'm checking to be sure she's not reading over my shoulder.)

So I called Izzy. She didn't come. Big surprise. I knew she was pretending not to hear me (this dog who hears us opening a bag of tortilla chips from half a house away). She was stalling for time. Weighing her options. I called her again, louder, and after a moment I heard the soft thump-thump as she landed, first on the couch, then on the floor. She walked into the kitchen and stopped, looking at me as I stood fifteen feet away in the back hall.

"Izzy, come," I said. My dog was a statue. She stared past me.

"Izzy! Come!" *You talking to me?* I repeated the command a fifth time. She cocked her head. *Eh? No speaka da English.*

I knelt down on the floor and patted the tile. "Izzy, come," I cooed. The sixth time's a charm. She started to move toward me, slo-o-owly, her tail tucked and head down. She can look so pathetic at times.

She was within a foot of me. "In your room," I said, pointing into the half bath off the hallway—"her" room. She stared at me, a look of pleading in her little black eyes. *Oh, please let me stay out here . . .*

"In your room," I ordered again. She backed up a step, looked away from me. I saw the muscles in her shoulders twitch. She was getting ready to bolt. I had to act fast.

"Sit!" I hollered. I shocked her into sitting. Before she could change her mind, I scooped her up, deposited her into her room, and set the baby gate in the bathroom doorway. "Good dog," I said. *Yeah right.* Sometimes I wonder who is really in charge around my house.

With Izzy secured, I sat at the kitchen table with a hot cup of coffee. It was quiet time at last.

I looked out the window. No breeze stirred the nearly bare oaks. No rustling critters—no squirrels, no chipmunks, not even a bird—disturbed the scene. I was alone. And it was quiet. Even the refrigerator was silent, not emitting any of its usual groans and hisses.

I savored the silence for just a moment, when I heard a woman shouting: *You're wasting time. You've got so much to do! Get busy!*

What horrible tyrant was screaming these orders at me? Why did she sound just like me? Who was this shrew living in my head?

"Hush!" I told her. "I *am* busy!"

You don't have time to waste like this, she started again. *Do something! Get to work!*

"Hush!" I said, louder this time. "I *am* doing something! I'm sitting here with God . . ."

I need this quiet time. I need to just sit sometimes and rest my body and mind. No question, it's hard to do, but it is *so* worth the effort. I crave the restorative boost I'm discovering in the quiet, in the silence, alone with God.

I need to take time to do "nothing" in the presence of God—not studying the Bible, not writing in my journal, not recording my "progress" on a chart, not reading inspirational books—just sitting with God. Just being there, not structuring every moment with God like I structure the rest of my life, but just being with him.

This activity has a technical name: meditation. Richard Foster says, in *Celebration of Discipline*, that meditation leads us into "detachment from the confusion all around us in order to have a richer attachment to God." Meditation is "the one thing that can sufficiently redirect our lives so that we can deal with human life successfully."

Meditation is the contemplation of God, thinking about the fact of his existence, the wonder of his love, the holiness of his nature, and the glory of his presence. What a stunning thing it is to be able to do that, to be *allowed* to contemplate a holy God! So why is it so hard for me to do this wonderful thing?

The apostle Peter wrote, "Be clear minded and self-controlled so that you can pray" (1 Peter 4:7). Peter hit on two of my biggest challenges. Being clear minded requires sweeping my mind clear of all the distractions: the dirty dishes, the dog shots, the dentist appointments. It means silencing my inner shrew.

Self-controlled? I've never been able to stay on task for long, unless I'm involved in something I really enjoy—spending time with friends and eating fudge, for instance. Was it possible that time with God didn't *have* to be a chore but could be as enjoyable as time with a friend? Was it possible I could feel a fudge-lover's kind of ardor for time with God?

Could time with God be something to look forward to—something I *want* to do instead of something I *have* to do? Foster seemed to think so. He and thousands, maybe millions, of other people found it wonderful to spend time with God. One of the keys seemed to be this doing nothing, this meditation.

Meditation is another way to worship. "Worship the Lord" always sounded so serious to me, an activity reserved for cathedrals with ornately carved high ceilings and stained-glass window panels. My cathedral is my kitchen. I worship the God of the universe at the altar of my kitchen table, with the jelly stuck to the place mats and faint impressions in the wood where a child did his homework and pressed a little too hard with the pen.

The kitchen ceiling isn't carved, only cobwebbed. The light fixture above the table isn't a crystal chandelier but a clearance-shelf bargain from the local home-improvement store. The window glass isn't leaded, only laden with the grime of a family's living.

But my kitchen table is where I meet God in the morning. Where I lift up my voice and sing songs of gratitude and praise. Where I sense him smiling as he listens. It's also where I sit in silence, listening to what he has to say about what he's done and who he is.

> *Able.* "Jesus looked at them intently and said, 'Humanly speaking, it is impossible. But with God everything is possible'" (Matthew 19:26 NLT). Is there anything I need that isn't included in "everything"?
>
> *Faithful.* "Never will I leave you; never will I forsake you" (Hebrews 13:5). Never. Never. Never.
>
> *Friend.* Jesus defined the term: "Greater love has no one than this, that he lay down his life for his friends" (John 15:13). He did just that for me. And for you.

Someone told me once, "If you want to hear from God, put yourself in a position to hear from him." That's what I'm learning to do in my kitchen cathedral. I'm learning to put myself in a position to hear from God. To obey his voice when he calls, "Come!" To obey his urging to just sit and stay a while, to be quiet and listen.

Sometimes he softly whispers words of love to my heart. I am loved. I am his. Sometimes he states a clear direction for the day, prompting me to call someone, to pray for someone, to go somewhere, or to tackle a particular task. Sometimes he causes an awareness of his presence—a tingling rush of his spirit that excites and energizes me at the same time it comforts and soothes me.

Sometimes, as on that gray October morning, he directs my attention to the wonders of his creation outside the window. The rush of a sudden wind rattling the oaks, the last leaves being shaken loose and falling, dying. The world white with early, unexpected snow, like forgiveness. And buried deep, the hope of spring and resurrection.

Don't you know that you yourselves are God's temple and that God's Spirit lives in you?

—1 Corinthians 3:16

points to ponder

1. When was the last time you sat in silence? How difficult was it for you? Try one minute of silence right now. How was it?

2. Where is your cathedral? Describe what happens when you enter that space.

3. What do you appreciate most about God? Think about that, talking to God about it, for a set time. (If you've never done this before, try three minutes to start. Set a timer so you won't be distracted.)

finding the way home

The letter from my father, the American soldier, to his brother back home was written June 4, 1945, from Camp Lucky Strike at Saint-Vallery, France. Almost a year after D-day. The long war was almost over. Tens of thousands of service personnel waited to be processed through the "cigarette camps" as World War II ended. Camp Lucky Strike was the primary camp for liberated American prisoners of war. My father was one of them. He'd been a prisoner of war, half-starved. He'd been set free. He was now waiting for his ride home.

While waiting, he wrote home to his older brother, the baker. My father wrote of his dreams, "nightly pilgrimages to the land where you so ably applied your skill, concocting and surrounding yourself with chocolate éclairs, cream puffs, Danish pastries . . ." The dreams, he wrote, "find me drooling when awakened by the morning bugle call."

My dad was hungry. Hungry for donuts. Hungry for home.

Where is home for you? Is there a place on earth that calls to your heart, a place that feels like home?

For Scarlett O'Hara in *Gone with the Wind*, it was the red earth of Tara that called to her. Trapped in Atlanta, war raging around her, hysterical Scarlett cries to Rhett Butler, "I want my mother. I want to go home to Tara!"

A friend of mine was raised in South America by her American missionary parents. They moved her back to their family home in Minnesota when she was a teenager, over twenty years ago. I asked her one day if Minnesota felt like home to her.

"No, it's too cold here," she said. "Urubamba will always be home to me. I wish I could go back and live there."

"Do you think the Midwest will ever feel like home?" I asked.

"Never," she said. "It feels like penance." One woman's paradise is another's punishment.

Where do you feel at home? My daughter Lizz loves all things Irish and dreams of going to Ireland, perhaps even living there. She is certain she was meant to be born there. Ireland calls to her. Alex, raised in Minnesota and California, has settled in between. He loves the rugged Colorado landscape and feels settled there in the Rockies. Son Dan thrives in the heart of Los Angeles, and daughter Laura prefers being near the ocean; she lives a few miles from the beach. For daughter Jenny, the desert feels like home. And Katy is content living a few miles from us in Wisconsin. This is home to her.

Where is home for you? Mountains or prairie? Ocean or desert? Forest or farmland? Tundra or jungle? Have you ever passed through an area, looked around, and wondered, *Why would anybody want to live here?* Too wet, too dry, too hot, too cold, too crowded, too deserted for me! We can't imagine how such a place could ever call to anyone's heart. How ironic that at the same time, others can't imagine how we can stand to live where we live.

Home is where the heart is, they say. We may take up residence in other places temporarily, but they don't ever quite *feel* like home, no matter how long we live there. I enjoyed my years in the desert of the Southwest, living with palm trees and cacti, sunshine and lack of humidity. I enjoyed being in a relatively bug-free zone; I most certainly did not miss mosquitoes. But for all the comforts and weather advantages, I never felt at home there.

I told you earlier about that weekend in California when I attended the women's retreat in the mountains. I was outside early on Saturday morning, sitting on a large boulder next to a mountain stream. As the cold, clear water rushed over the rocks, I breathed deeply the sweet scent of pines and snow.

I realized in that moment that where we lived—the heat, the smog, the dust—would never feel like home. I needed clear, blue, smogless sky. I needed green rolling farm fields and forests. I needed pine trees and water. I needed seasons that change. I needed snow in the winter. I needed *my* Urubamba. I needed *my* Tara. (I needed *my* mommy!) I needed to go home.

We become so attached to the places we love, don't we? In the movie version of *Gone with the Wind*, Scarlett's father, Gerald O'Hara, taught her that land was "the only thing in the world worth working for, worth fighting for, worth dying for, because it's the only thing that lasts."

Mr. O'Hara, I respectfully disagree. As wonderful as home and property may be, this world—and everything about our earthly home—is just temporary.

Our real, everlasting home is elsewhere. We live now in shadow, seeing through a glass darkly, partially sighted, with limited vision. We exist in twilight, in fog, in this interval of time between birth and death, here on this planet, in this place. But it's only temporary.

Have you sensed it too? Recognized the fleetingness of this life? In the quiet moments, when you're alone, have you realized the temporary nature of relationships, houses, and possessions? In the stillness, have you sensed the calling of your own heart toward something more permanent? Toward an eternal home?

I have. As a child, I asked questions while lying in bed at night, alone in the dark. Perhaps you did too. *Why am I here? What's this life all about?* I felt an intense longing, like homesickness, as if I didn't belong here. God calls to us. He creates in every one of us a sensitive and alive spiritual core—a *knowing* of where we belong. A homing beacon directing us to our true home: God's heart.

Zelda died last year. Sweet, sweet Zelda, who supplied the Thanksgiving meal, who was the grandmother of my friend Charlene, who directed me to the field of carrots. Generosity runs in the family. Zelda was a strong, faithful Christian who embodied the idea of "prayer warrior," though she would humbly deny it. Zelda prayed. After Zelda died, Charlene said she could tell her grandmother was no longer praying.

"Who is going to pray for our family now?" Charlene wondered. I wonder who will miss my prayers when I die. Who will miss yours?

Zelda's health had been declining for years. She was tired, she told her family. Is there a time when we get to say, "Lord, I'm tired and I want to come home now"? Is there a time when, having prayed for a lifetime, we can say to family and friends, "I'm done praying for all of you. You're going to have to take over now because I'm going home"? The apostle Paul said he "would prefer to be away from the body and at home with the Lord" (2 Corinthians 5:8). Zelda may have felt the same way.

I've never been to a funeral at which I was more certain that it was a celebration. We all knew where Zelda had gone. She'd gone home. The funeral was a joyful celebration of a beautiful woman's life. There was deep sadness at having to part, no question, but also joy for having known her, having been blessed to see her smile, to feel her warm embraces, to hear her sweet prayers. And a joyful certainty—gladness for her—that she had, at last, her heart's desire. That she was indeed "at home with the Lord."

That desire for our real home, that longing, is a beacon through the fog, shining our way back to the safety of the harbor, shining through the dark, across the miles, calling us home. The beacon searches us out and draws us back, no matter how far we've drifted off course. The light draws us—travelers passing through this world—back home. It shines the way until our restless wandering is settled, at last, by the sight of God.

Where is home? Home is where everybody knows your name. Home is the family reunion where, no matter how long you've been gone, how far you've wandered, or what you've been doing, you are recognized and you are welcome. Home is, no matter how far you've traveled, always home.

I drove home one day at the end of a long road trip. My legs cramped from too many hours in the car, my hands tired from gripping the wheel, I turned down the road a couple of miles from our house. I recognized the dairy farm, the apple orchard, the red barn tilting behind the white frame house.

As I turned onto the road in our neighborhood, I recognized smaller details—the wooden plaque with the pheasant decal hanging next to one neighbor's driveway. The planter full of morning glories winding up the mailbox post of another neighbor's house.

As I crested the hill on our road, my heart skipped a little. *Home is just around this bend.* The house came into view. Our house. Our burgundy shutters. Our garden. Our hostas. Our echinacea.

Home.

Back at Camp Lucky Strike in 1945, my father looked forward to going home, to being reunited with those he loved. He wrote in that letter, "I don't know exactly to the day when we shall take leave of this place, but I do know that we shall embark from here for Home Sweet Home. I pray it's very soon."

Isn't that how it is for God's children? We don't know the exact date or the hour, but the day is coming—and what a glorious day it will be—when we, after a life of longing, shall certainly embark from here, bound for the grandest reunion of all time: the gathering of God's family, all the generations, together.

We'll round the last bend and a voice—a most familiar voice—will whisper, "Welcome home."

And we will be home—sweet home—at last.

I write these things to you who believe in the name of the Son of God so that you may know that you have eternal life.

—1 John 5:13

points to ponder

1. How many times have you moved in your life? Describe the worst and the best of your moving experiences. Where is paradise for you? Where would you *not* want to live? Why not?

2. Have you known anyone like Zelda? Describe her (or him). What impact has your "Zelda" had in your life?

3. Have you heard the saying "You can't go home again"? Do you agree or disagree? Explain your answer. What do you think it means to be "at home with the Lord"? Is there an eternal home for you?

you've come a long way, baby

I've come a long way. A long, lo-o-ong way. Wife, mommy, grandma, sister, daughter, and friend. Teacher, stockbroker, success, and failure. Fat, thin, fatter, thinner, and everything in between. Poor and slightly less poor. Younger and firmer, now older and flabbier.

I've hugged my inner child. I've embraced my inner Mrs. Potato Head. I've forgiven my inner giant for turning out to be a wimp. I've surrendered my illusions, my kids, and my metal bra.

I've weathered storms—listened to the thunder, been drenched in the driving rain. I've crossed deserts—buffeted by hot, dry wind and thirsting for hope. I've seen war and peace (never read it, but I've lived it).

I've lived life, loved and lost, laughed and cried, for more decades than I care to count. I've been around long enough to see miniskirts and bell-bottoms return to fashion! Alas, by the time the fads of our youth come back in style, we're too old to wear them. Then again, I didn't look that great in them the first time around.

I've been, seen, and done so much. And I'm not done yet.

Life, space for living, is just opening up. Older children equal a roomier nest. Letting go of the clutter—the junk, the attitudes, the past—frees a lot of physical, mental, and emotional space. New adventures beckon. (I have rooms to redecorate!) New challenges await. (Long-distance biking? Snowboarding? But first, assembling the new hammock. It's all about priorities.)

So many great possibilities I don't know what to do first. Do you feel it too? Are you, like me, asking, "What now? What's next?"

Ask God. He knows.

When King David passed the torch to his son Solomon, recounted in 1 Chronicles 28:9–10, he offered this direction: "And you, my son Solomon, acknowledge the God of your father, and serve him with wholehearted devotion and with a willing mind, for the LORD searches every heart and understands every motive behind the thoughts. If you seek him, he will be found by you; but if you forsake him, he will reject you forever. Consider now, for the LORD has chosen you to build a temple as a sanctuary. Be strong and do the work."

Great advice.

1. Acknowledge God

Recognize the God who created you, he who "rides the ancient skies" (Psalm 68:33) and "rides on the wings of the wind" (Psalm 104:3). Creator, Sustainer, immortal, invisible God. He is the one who loves you with an everlasting love. He's seen you at your best and at your worst.

Acknowledge God. As you know if you've read Psalm 139, God knows when you sleep, when you rise, when you come in, and when you go out. He is the one who let you wake up this morning. He saw you this morning as you rolled out of bed, with the clump of hair sticking out, your eyes barely open, stumbling toward the bathroom. He loved you even then. Before you washed your face and combed your hair. Before you brushed your teeth. Eww. Doesn't that deserve a little gratitude?

Before you were born, he ordained your days, numbered each one. He's been there, with you, every moment of every day. He saw you, in fact, before you were even conceived. He imagined you back then. Imagine that! You are his creation, his work of art—cellulite and all.

And you are wonderful—an amazing complex system of bone, sinew, tissue, organ, thought, feeling, need, and will, firing on all cylinders (more or less). Moving. Thinking. Laughing. Loving. You are a miracle. God does nice work. That's worth a thank-you, don't you think?

Acknowledge him. He let you draw the breath you just took. Think about what it took to do that. The lungs, the nasal passages, those little wiggly things that filter the junk out of the air. Incredible, the way the system works. And you don't give it a thought, do you? He lets you breathe. God lets you breathe. By his grace, he lets you keep on breathing. You might want to thank him for that.

The almighty Creator, eternal God, cares about the details of your life. He cares deeply about how you spend the time you've been allotted. Acknowledge him. Faithless and wandering though we may be, he brings us back, rescuing us as many times as we need it. He is the faithful one, a true promise keeper. That's praiseworthy, don't you think?

Acknowledge God. Thank him for all he has done. Thank him for the difference he's making in your life right now. Transforming, renewing, saving. Making you alive. Alive!

Acknowledge God. Bless his holy name.

2. Serve Him with Wholehearted Devotion

David encourages Solomon to have passion. Passion about following God's leading. It's easy to be passionate when you are young and full of energy, passionate about getting your education or starting a new career. Where is the passion when the job's a dead end? When they're not hiring in your field?

It's easy to be passionate about a new marriage or having babies. Where is the passion when the kids are grown and gone? Where is the passion we used to feel for that shapeless lump in the recliner with the remote in a death grip? For the shapeless lump we've become?

Whatever you do, do it for God. He will supply the passion. Rework your résumé. Rework your life. Hug the lump. Do the work. Wholeheartedly. With passion. For God.

3. Serve Him with a Willing Mind

Be open to God's leading. It's easy for me to become set in my ways and say, "This is the way I've always done it, and I'm not changing. It's my way or the highway." It's hard work overcoming inertia, fighting the friction that keeps us from moving forward. But our infinitely creative Father has new plans, fresh ideas, and exciting adventures in mind for us—if we are willing to go along with his plans.

Will yourself to be willing. "Forget the former things; do not dwell on the past. See, I am doing a new thing! Now it springs up; do you not perceive it? I am making a way in the desert and streams in the wasteland" (Isaiah 43:18–19).

Do you perceive new things on your horizon? What new thing does God have in mind for you? Open your mind.

Complete this sentence ten different ways: "If I had the time and the money, I would ..." What's stopping you? Which one of those things seems possible? How might you start?

4. Seek Him and Find Him

Seek God, David tells his son, and warns him not to forsake God and risk his rejection. Seek God. You've said no to some things. Now you have time to seek the Lord, time to get that Bible dirty. Time to pray those prayers. Time to receive his healing of the past. Time to forgive and move forward. It's time. So seek. Find.

5. Consider

Think! This is a huge challenge for me these days, when my brain has turned to oatmeal. (*Think? Huh?*) But the mind, science says, is like a muscle: use it or lose it. Contrary to the evidence in my life, there is no age limit on how much the brain can absorb or for how long. Research shows that the memory part of the brain does *not* lose nerve cells as we age and can actually produce new ones. That's why it's never too late to learn.

"Sixty is the new thirty," I've heard. "Seventy is relatively young," says another expert. "People should be prepared for a long, productive life." How old are you? Do you have a ten-year plan? How about a fifty-year plan? Better to have a plan and not need it than to need a plan and not have one!

Keep learning. Did you know that the average undergraduate adult learner in America is almost forty years old? One woman started working on her college degree via the Internet at the age of fifty. A fifty-nine-year-old woman received her degree and invited her three grandchildren to walk across the platform with her. My friend started a master's program at fifty-five. "In five years, I'll be sixty," she said. "I figured I'd rather be sixty *with* a master's degree than sixty *without* one!" Why not? As the saying goes, "It's never too late to be what you might have been." Never too late.

Solomon knew what he was supposed to do: build the temple as a sanctuary for the Lord. What is God asking you to do? Think. Fill in the blank for yourself:

"Consider now, for the Lord has chosen you to _____
_____."

God has certainly given you gifts and talents. What are you good at? Ask those close to you to give you insight into the gifts and talents they see in you.

What is the Lord choosing you to do these days? Some friends of ours recently retired from their corporate jobs and joined a missionary organization. They're having the time of their lives. A young mother began a quilt ministry, enlisting her quilting friends to make and donate small quilts to comfort children with life-threatening diseases at her local children's hospital.

A widow I know has opened her home to single pregnant women who are choosing to carry their babies to term rather than aborting them. She's offering these women shelter and comfort during a difficult time. She's even saving lives.

Think. Consider. Is there a homeless shelter, a cancer unit, or a nursing home longing for your good cheer? Think about your gifts. Think about what you've enjoyed in the past, what you've always wished you could do—if only you had the time. Do you have the time now?

Consider. Think. What has the Lord chosen *you* to do?

6. Be Strong

I make the calls on my birthday each year: I call my doctor to schedule my yearly checkup. I call the hospital to schedule my annual mammogram. I call the dentist to confirm my routine checkup and cleaning appointment.

Be strong, the Bible says. Be physically strong. Lift, bend, stretch, pedal, walk, hike, run. To keep going, to keep doing all that needs to be done, we need to be able to breathe, to move, and to lift.

Never exercised before? Check with your doctor and start. Need to lose some weight? Check with your doctor and start. I saw a poster in the local hospital's cardiac care unit. Under a picture of a bratwurst in a bun (the unofficial state food in Wisconsin, along with cheese and beer), a caption explained that eight million bratwursts would be consumed in the next year in Wisconsin. The poster asked, "Aren't you glad to have high-quality cardiac care in the neighborhood?"

Glad indeed, but I'll be even gladder not to *need* high-quality cardiac care in my own or any other neighborhood.

I may never run a marathon, but I can walk a little farther this week than I did last week. I may never pump iron (unless the steam iron counts), but I can lift a few pounds a few times this week. (Is that a bicep beginning to bulge?) I may never be able to assume a lotus position without hearing the snap, crackle, and pop of my knees and hips, but I can stretch a little now and then. (I can see my toes—that's progress. Maybe one day I'll touch them again. A girl can dream.)

My new motto for exercising: Something is better than nothing.

Be strong, the Bible says. Be mentally strong. Mental strength is focus. Over the years I've had to make my job—writing—fit in with my life. I've studied the books and listened to the advice: Write first thing in the morning. Write every day. Write on a schedule. Write all the time. Find what works for you and go with that. So much advice about writing. I studied it all—and studied it, and studied it. I spent a lot of time studying about writing, thinking about writing, talking to friends about writing. I spent very little time actually writing! One day I decided that I was tired of reading about how other people did it. I wanted to see some of my own dreams come true.

Self-discipline (ugh!) is the key. Not my strong suit, as you know. I'm learning to be disciplined, learning what it feels like to focus. It's not easy—it goes against every fiber of my being, actually—but by being more focused, by being more intentional about how I spend my time, some of my writing dreams are actually coming true. (You're holding one of them. Thank you!)

It's a whole lot of work to try to make your own dreams come true all by yourself. Why would we want to do that when omnipotent God is ready to help us?

God provides. *Lord, give me the mind and hands of a writer today. Give me the skill of a Martha at home this morning. Give me the heart of a servant for this meeting. Give me the compassion of a ministering angel for this hurting friend. Give me the patience of a saint with the grandchildren today.*

Be strong, the Bible says. Strong with the strength and focus God provides.

7. Do the Work

The point of spending quality time with God is to be equipped to get out there and share his love with the rest of the world. So get to work. Don't just talk about the work, think about the work, or dream about the work. *Do* the work, and as you do, remember, "It is God who works in you to will and to act according to his good purpose" (Philippians 2:13).

Do the work God has given you to do. Get on with the work of life. What changes do you want to make? Who can help you? When will you start? Where will you find what you need? How can you pursue God's best for you?

Get on with it. Make your plan. Jump on the wagon. Dive into the fray. Roll up your sleeves. Get your hands dirty.

Get that degree. Find that new job. Rock those babies. Join that community organization. Write the book. Volunteer for the church nursery. Sing in the choir. Serve meals to the homeless. Visit the prisoner. Comfort the sick. Help the needy.

Tutor a child. Help out in the classroom. Take a class and learn to draw, to dance, to throw a pot. Teach a class and share your talents.

Let go of the past. Grieve what you must and then move on. Embrace the future. Mend a fence. Forgive a hurt. Make peace.

Accept others. Expect less from them. Give more to them.

In whatever you do, acknowledge the God who made you. Seek him and serve him willingly, wholeheartedly, and thoughtfully. Be strong—physically, mentally, emotionally, and spiritually—with the strength he provides.

You've come a long way, baby, but you're not done yet. Almighty God has plans for you. Go and do what he has chosen you to do.

May he bless you as you go and do, and may he give you the desires of your heart. And when he comes to take you home, may he find you smack in the middle of things—still serving him and still seeking him, with wholehearted devotion.

Now put this book down and get going!

> Teach me your way, O Lord,
>   and I will walk in your truth;
> give me an undivided heart,
>   that I may fear your name.
>   —Psalm 86:11

When Did I Stop Being Barbie and Become Mrs. Potato Head?

Learning to Embrace the Woman You've Become

Mary Pierce

Embrace Your Inner Mrs. Potato Head!

She's so much more real and full of fun than Barbie ever could be. And she knows how to laugh like only those who have discovered the humor, heart, and wisdom of true womanhood can laugh. Give her room to romp with this hilarious collection of zany, true-life stories by Mary Pierce.

If you love to kick off your shoes and laugh your socks off over the foibles and absurdities of life, this book is for you. Mrs. Potato Head's hormones are out of whack. Her memory is held together by sticky notes. But she's got a sense of humor that just won't quit, and she's learned to accept and enjoy herself as she is—because God does.

Softcover: 0-310-24856-6